BISON
BOOKS

D0825451

To Hell

Dans l'enfer des tournantes

FRANCE OVERSEAS:
Studies in Empire and Decolonization

SERIES EDITORS:
*Philip Boucher, A. J. B. Johnston,
James D. Le Sueur, and Tyler Stovall*

and Back

The Life of Samira Bellil

Samira Bellil

TRANSLATED BY LUCY R. MCNAIR

INTRODUCTION BY ALEC G. HARGREAVES

University of Nebraska Press | Lincoln

Publication of this book was assisted by a grant from the National Endowment for the Arts.

NATIONAL ENDOWMENT FOR THE ARTS
A great nation deserves great art.

LIBRARY OF CONGRESS
CATALOGING-IN-PUBLICATION DATA

Bellil, Samira.
 [Dans l'enfer des tournantes. English]
 To hell and back : the life of Samira Bellil / Samira Bellil ; translated by Lucy R. McNair ; introduction by Alec G. Hargreaves.
   p.   cm.
 ISBN 978-0-8032-1356-2 (pbk. : alk. paper)
 1. Bellil, Samira. 2. Rape victims—France—Biography. 3. Muslim women—France—Biography. I. Title.
 HV6569.F8B4513 2008
 362.883092—dc22   [B] 2008005510

Set in Adobe Garamond by Bob Reitz. Designed by A. Shahan.

reputation: manner in which a person or thing is considered.

Larousse Encyclopedic Dictionary

reputation: status attributed to a person by rampant word-of-mouth transmission, an image inseparable from that person, which, in every instance, shatters lives—whether you're a gangster, a goon or a "cellar slut."

Dictionary of Street Talk

Contents

Acknowledgments

To my sisters in distress, to show them it's possible to make it out. It's long and difficult, but it can be done.

To my family.

To my sisters Mejda and Assïa—I love you.

To Papa Jean, Mama Josette, Toon, Vinaye, and Vimala—for the happiness I learned among you.

Deep gratitude to three people who supported my rebirth: To Fanny, for rescuing me from hell and helping me to become a real person; to Josée, for her warmth, attention, and support throughout the writing of this book and who, with great finesse, knew how to polish my writing while respecting it; to my lawyer, for attempting "the impossible" and succeeding. Thank you for these magnificent gifts.

Thanks to Boris Cyrulnik for his book *Merveilleux malheur* [*Marvelous Misfortune*], which gave me a ton of hope.

Special thanks to: Insaf (alias The Giraffe) and crazy Benoît: "Your endless capacity to love others surprises me every day"; Teresa and her family: "I'm waiting for you!"; Fabiola, alias Madame Fifi II; Memed, "for your bullet-proof love!"; Franck, Nacim, Fred, David, and all those I met at your home; Dourdin, my Roman; Malek, "You know . . ."; Totof, Kalhilou, Pishcal; Don Jambone and his l'il bro who finally grew up!; Mektoub and his family; Kader; Lydia; Sabrina; Redha; Raquel; DDF and the others. Cyril the cute kid; Virginie "The Lady of the Night!" and Luis from Corch Valley; Jean-Claude my cruise doc!! Thanks for your support, your love, and your unshakable spirits.

And finally, thanks to all those who smiled at me one day or held out a friendly hand just when I needed it most.

Introduction

ALEC G. HARGREAVES

Samira Bellil's story is deeply disturbing on multiple levels. It begins with the gang rape that Bellil suffered at the age of fourteen and then traces the devastating impact it had on her adolescence and early adulthood. These harrowing experiences raise troubling questions about the environment in which they occur, the socially disadvantaged multiethnic urban areas known in France as the *banlieues*. When the narrative was first published in 2002, it became a symbol of abuses suffered by women in the banlieues and of their determination to fight against those abuses. At the same time, media coverage given to the book raised fears that minority ethnic women who, like Bellil, spoke out against such abuses ran the risk of being manipulated by politicians and journalists, generating misleading ethnic stereotypes that stigmatize minorities of recent immigrant origin, especially those of Muslim heritage.

Samira Bellil was born in 1972 in Algeria. Her parents had also been born there but as young adults had emigrated to France, where they had met and married. Both had suffered physical abuse as children. In the face of family disapproval of their marriage, they moved several times between France and Algeria, settling in France shortly after the birth of Samira. At about the same time, Samira's father was given a five-year jail sentence for offences committed in France, the precise nature of which is not indicated in Bellil's narrative. In her husband's absence, Samira's mother went out to work full time and, unable to take care of her daughter, placed her with foster parents in Belgium, where Samira lived most of her early childhood, returning at the age of five to the family home in the banlieues of Paris. It is there, in the *département* (county) of Seine-Saint-Denis, to the northeast of central Paris, that most of the events described in the narrative take place.

The banlieues are in many ways a world apart from the older and generally more affluent neighborhoods of downtown Paris, to which the narrative takes us only fleetingly during sporadic visits to cheap nightclubs and similar venues on the northern edge of the central part of the capital, as well as when Bellil changes trains at the Gare-du-Nord station, a central hub linking the downtown metro with several RER (express metro) lines running out into the northern and eastern banlieues of Paris.[1] In its sprawling high-rise tower blocks of subsidized social housing, typical of the banlieues, Seine-Saint-Denis contains greater concentrations of poverty and of minority ethnic groups than any other département in France. According to police data, it also contains some of the nation's most violent neighborhoods, with especially high rates of homicide and armed robbery.[2] In addition, recent research indicates that more than one in ten young women in Seine-Saint-Denis may have been subject to sexual assaults, with one in four having suffered other types of physical assault.[3]

Compared with the "ghettos" of American cities, which are often populated almost entirely by a single minority ethnic group (typically, African Americans or Hispanics), the banlieues of Paris in which Bellil's story unfolds, like those of other French cities, are relatively diverse in their ethnic composition. While home to dense populations of immigrant origin, they also contain a significant proportion of majority ethnic residents. The largest of the minority ethnic groups come from the former French North African colonies of Algeria, Morocco, and Tunisia, while others originate in the parts of sub-Saharan Africa, the Caribbean, and Asia that were formerly colonized by France. Most of these territories gained independence from France in the 1950s and early 1960s. During the economic boom years that followed the Second World War, migrants from impoverished colonies or former colonies took up low-paid, unskilled jobs in metropolitan France, where there were serious labor shortages. Initially, their families generally remained in their countries of origin, but this changed amid the oil crises of the 1970s. Fearing rising unemployment, the French government banned fresh labor migrants from outside Europe and attempted to repatriate those already in the country. These efforts backfired, leading many migrants to conclude that during a period of economic insecurity it would be unwise to risk leaving France. Instead, they now brought their families to France and established the permanent settlement of new immigrant minorities.[4]

The Bellil family was part of this demographic shift. Although Samira was born slightly before the 1974 ban on labor migration from outside Europe, she and her younger sisters, born in France in the 1980s, were part of the second generation of North Africans, who became increasingly visible during this period. In the course of these events, a new appellation—*Beurs*—became widely applied to them.[5] The Bellils were not in every respect typical of immigrant families from North Africa. There were only three children (about half the average for such families), their income level was sufficient to allow the Bellils to buy their home instead of renting the kind of low-cost social housing in which immigrant families were generally concentrated, and they had the means to send Samira to a privately run Catholic school for at least part of her education. But the neighborhoods in which they lived sat cheek by jowl with the high-rise housing projects that dominate the banlieues of Paris. Frustrated with the restrictions imposed on her at home, the adolescent Bellil spent much of her time hustling on the streets of the banlieues, where she mixed with young people typical of this disadvantaged milieu. Her narrative is peppered with slang and swearwords picked up as part of the daily currency of life on those streets where colloquial French is mixed with terms from Arabic and other immigrant-borne languages and with liberal borrowings from rap and other forms of youth culture originating in the United States.[6]

During the 1980s and 1990s, unemployment in France escalated rapidly. The simultaneous rise of new immigrant minorities in the banlieues led a growing part of the population to believe the propaganda of the extreme-right Front National, according to which immigrants from former colonies were to blame not only for rising unemployment but also for virtually every other ill afflicting the nation. In reality, discrimination against non-Europeans was so rife that they suffered much higher levels of unemployment than the majority ethnic population. Bellil's father was among those who, from the mid-1980s onward, languished in long-term unemployment. Unemployment rates went higher still among second-generation North Africans. These rates exceeded 40 percent during the 1990s, compared with a peak of 13 percent among the national population.[7]

Discrimination has often been fueled by Islamophobia directed against postcolonial minorities, the largest of which come from predominantly Islamic countries in North Africa. Second-and third-generation members of these minorities, born and raised in France, are generally less attached to Islam than their parents; but this has not prevented them from being stigmatized and discriminated against by members of the majority ethnic population, leading to deep resentment and upsurges of violence among younger residents of the banlieues.

Seine-Saint-Denis was the epicenter of the riots that tore through the banlieues of numerous French cities in November 2005, the nation's most serious civil disturbances in almost forty years. While unprecedented in scale, such riots were not in themselves new. At a lower level of intensity, similar disturbances had been occurring since the late 1970s in the banlieues, where mainly young minority ethnic men were pitted against police officers seen as representatives of an unjust and repressive social order. This dynamic was in many ways encapsulated in Matthieu Kassovitz's films *La Haine* (1995), the title of which means "*The Hate*" and refers to the hatred or rage felt by young men in the banlieues in the face of police harassment, perceived as emblematic of their victimization by mainstream French society.

In her narrative, Bellil often speaks of a similar feeling of hate, but it is directed primarily against those who are located within the banlieues, rather than outside of them. The rage she feels is against those who raped her and against all those in the banlieues who subsequently shunned or mistreated her as if the rape constituted an ongoing license to abuse her. Profoundly gendered, Bellil's personal experience is also deeply imbricated by wider social tensions. Young rioters in the banlieues are almost exclusively male, as are members of the gangs that often seek to dominate public spaces there. In some cases, gang members and other young men have been tempted to assuage the frustration arising from their exclusion from mainstream French society by victimizing "soft" targets, especially women, inside the banlieues. This has generated among their victims comparable feelings of rage toward their assailants and those whom they feel side with them.

The phenomenon known colloquially in the banlieues as *tournantes* (gang rapes) were first brought to public attention in the year 2000 by the movie *La Squale* (*The Tearaway*). The first to be signed by a victim of a tournante, Bellil's narrative was published in 2002, a few weeks after the death of seventeen-year-old Sohane Benziane, who was burned alive in the banlieue of Vitry-sur-Seine by a nineteen-year-old youth. Amid the wave of publicity generated by Benziane's death and the publication of Bellil's story, seen as symptomatic of violence against women endemic in the banlieues, a group of minority ethnic women led by Fadila Amara launched a movement called *Ni putes ni soumises* (Neither sluts nor slaves), designed to prevent similar abuses in the future. Bellil agreed to serve as its honorary president.[8]

Ni putes ni soumises quickly gained support among politicians across a broad swathe of the party spectrum. Among them was Jean-Louis Debré, center-right president of the National Assembly. Working with Ni putes ni soumises to mark Bastille Day on July 14, 2003, Debré arranged for the facade of the National Assembly, overlooking the river Seine across from the Place de la Concorde, to be covered by huge photographs of fourteen young women from the banlieues described as "Mariannes d'aujourd'hui" (Mariannes for Today). Bellil was among the women whose images were displayed in this way. On one level, Debré's initiative could be perceived as a long overdue recognition of the status of minority ethnic women as full citizens of the French Republic, which since the revolution of 1789 has been incarnated in the mythical but habitually white figure of Marianne. On another level, however, some saw in the photographs a manipulative form of paternalism in which women of Muslim heritage were portrayed as being protected by the Republic from Islamic misogyny allegedly enveloping the banlieues.[9] Only a few years earlier, while serving as interior minister, Debré had earned notoriety by sending in riot police to haul minority ethnic women and children out of the churches in which they had sought sanctuary in the face of a new law preventing them from acquiring residence permits in France. Debré's new alliance with Ni putes ni soumises had the benefit of softening his public image, in which he now appeared as the defender of women's rights.

Bellil, like Amara, was often accused of playing into the hands of reactionaries and Islamophobes because of her public denunciation of violence inflicted on women in the banlieues.[10] Both women were in fact always careful to avoid attributing violence in the banlieues to Islamic culture per se or to Muslim men in general, but this was often lost in media coverage of tournantes, which were commonly presented as a form of abuse inflicted by Muslim men on Muslim women and thereby as indicative of unacceptable tendencies inherent in Islam.[11] As she shows in the later part of her narrative, Bellil was well aware of the dangers of media manipulations, which she did her best to resist. Like several other young women authors of Muslim heritage, she was assisted in writing her narrative by a professional journalist. Through this process, these women often appear to have lost control of their stories to sensationalist and sometimes Islamophobic editorial and publicity machines.[12] Bellil was relatively successful in using her collaborator, Josée Stoquart, to sharpen her prose and her self-image without allowing the text to be infiltrated by stereotypical images of Muslim culture. This did not prevent Stoquart from adding a preface to the book, in which she portrayed the sexual violence of young men in the banlieues as a consequence of their being caught between Islamic fundamentalism and the cheap pornography of Western consumer society.[13] Bellil's narrative made no reference to Islamic fundamentalism, but Stoquart's representation of events in those terms was given widespread currency by journalists, many of whom may have seen in the preface a shortcut that saved them the trouble of reading Bellil's text.[14]

Islam is not inherently misogynist, nor do its basic principles endorse the abuse of women. At the same time, it is unquestionably the case that women in Muslim societies are generally expected to behave in more reserved ways than men. Even when they are not the victims of physical abuse, young women of Muslim heritage in the banlieues often feel unfairly treated compared with their male peers, who tend to be allowed much greater personal freedom. Muslim parents are often preoccupied with protecting the virginity of their daughters prior to marriage, which they regard as a matter of honor. While sons are allowed to roam at will outside the family home, daughters may not be allowed out on their own and are often expected to perform domestic chores from which their brothers are excused. Bellil's mother attempted to inculcate in her daughter values of this kind, but the young Bellil's comings and goings were less rigidly policed than those of young women in other Muslim families, perhaps because the father's long absence from the family home during Bellil's early years made it harder for him to assert untrammeled authority over her. In addition, there were no brothers to serve as male proxies for her father. In her early teens, Bellil frequently ran away from home when her father tried to assert his authority. When living at home, she suffered at the hands of her father a disturbing combination of physical and verbal abuse alternating with bouts of contempt and neglect, notably following the gang rape. His harshness was indeed such that the adolescent Bellil was at times thrown out onto the streets, with all the dangers associated with this. Only a month after the gang rape, she was raped for a second time by the principal assailant in the initial attack.

There is little evidence of Islam having played a significant role in the behavior of Bellil's father and still less of it having motivated the young men who raped her. Bellil's narrative refers explicitly to Muslims only once, when discussing the importance attached to the virginity of women prior to marriage. Elsewhere, she refers in more general terms to the "traditions" or "culture" of her parents and their attempts to literally beat those traditions into her without a word of explanation. Neither her mother nor her father appears to have received much formal education. There is no reference to them observing Islamic practices such as regular prayers or fasting during Ramadan, nor is there any indication of their transmitting to Samira doctrinal knowledge about the teachings of Islam. The traditions that they attempt to inculcate into Samira no doubt reflect in part their understanding of Islam, especially where relations between the sexes are concerned; but the violent manner of the father is clearly rooted in the violence experienced during his own childhood rather than in any precepts to be found in Islamic scriptures. Bellil implicitly points to the un-Islamic nature of her father's behavior when she refers ironically to his way of "celebrating" Fridays, the holiest day of the week for Muslims, by getting drunk, in defiance of Islamic teachings forbidding alcohol, and beating her.

Similarly, Bellil sees the violence of young men in the banlieues as an extension of the tradition of machismo displayed by their fathers at home, a tradition that has little to do with Islamic teachings. She refers to those who raped her as "des gens de couleur" (people of color), a description that does not readily evoke Muslims. It suggests, indeed, that one or more of her assailants may not have been of North African descent but black, originating in sub-Saharan Africa or the Caribbean, a possibility concordant with the fact that Seine-Saint-Denis is home to many migrants from the French Caribbean départements of Martinique and Guadeloupe, where Catholicism is the dominant religion. None of this fits with the idea that the sexual abuse of women such as Bellil can be attributed to Islamic beliefs or culture.

In the postface to the first edition of her narrative, Bellil sums up her experiences as exemplifying the worst aspects of the banlieues, which are first and foremost a marginalized social space rather than a religious entity. This perspective is in line with the empirical evidence adduced by the sociologist Laurent Mucchielli, who has shown that while the nomenclature of tournantes is new, the phenomenon of gang rape is not. Neither is it unique to or especially preponderant among men of North African or Muslim heritage, nor are its victims to be found solely or even predominantly among those ethnic groups.[15] None of this is to reduce or excuse the heinous nature of the assaults suffered by Bellil. It is, however, important not to draw unwarranted inferences linking such attacks to the Muslim heritage shared by some (by no means all) residents of the banlieues.

If offences of this nature can be seen in part as an extension of violent reflexes among poorly educated fathers and in part as a reaction to the self-perception of young men as victims of social marginalization and police harassment, the effect of such assaults has been to create a further class of victims among the young women targeted for physical abuse. In attempting to surmount her traumatic experiences, Bellil in turn abused her own body with drugs, alcohol, and at least one suicide attempt. It was only in her late twenties that she was rescued from this spiral of violence by a form of psychotherapy that treated her body together with her mind. The writing of her narrative was a pivotal part of this therapy. Instead of trying to dull her memory and camouflage her pain through drugs, she resolved to try to understand her past by thinking and writing about it as lucidly as possible. If at times the text takes on a self-justificatory tone, it should not be forgot-

ten that until writing her narrative Bellil had frequently been surrounded by people who, instead of sympathizing with her plight,
blamed her for it.

Bellil conceived of writing as a way to cleanse herself of the pain
that for years had been bottled up within her. In the narrative she
speaks frequently of having felt as if her stomach had been tied
in knots or invaded by a ball of pain, likened at times to boiling
magma, triggering epileptic fits. In writing the book, she felt as
if she finally divested herself of this burden. Sadly, scarcely two
years after publishing the book, she died of stomach cancer. Her
death at the age of thirty-one makes Bellil's narrative all the more
poignant. It also makes it all the more important that as readers
we understand the nature of the cruel adversities that befell her
and the extraordinary resilience and determination Bellil showed
in trying to surmount them.

NOTES

1. On the social and ethnic diversity associated with the RER network linking the banlieues with downtown Paris, see François Maspéro, *Les Pas-
   sagers du Roissy-Express* (Paris: Seuil, 1990), translated by Paul Jones as
   Roissy Express: A Journey Through the Paris Suburbs (London: Verso, 1994).
2. Jean-Marc Leclerc, "Plongée au coeur de la cité la plus violente du '9–3,'"
   Le Figaro, June 12, 2007.
3. Luc Bronner, "Quatre jeunes filles sur dix ont été victimes de violences en
   Seine-Saint-Denis," *Le Monde*, March 8, 2007.
4. On postcolonial immigration and settlement in France, see Alec G. Hargreaves, *Multi-Ethnic France: Immigration, Politics, Culture and Society*
   (London: Routledge, 2007).
5. "Beur" and the feminine form "Beurette" are now commonly dismissed
   as labels by those to whom they are applied, including Bellil, who see in
   such labels cliché-ridden forms of marginalization.
6. On banlieue culture, see "Cities/Banlieues," eds. Roger Célestin, Eliane
   DalMolin and Alec G. Hargreaves, special issues, *Contemporary French*

and Francophone Studies 8, no. 1 (January 2004) and 8, no. 2 (Spring 2004). A prominent type of slang in the banlieues is *verlan* (backslang), formed by inverting the syllables of words. Widely used examples include *meuf*, an inversion of *femme* (woman), and *caillera*, an inversion of *racaille* (scum or street punk). The latter term has frequently been adopted as a self-designation by rebellious youths in the banlieues, including Bellil, as a way of recognizing and playing upon their stigmatized status. It is a form of self-affirmation comparable to that of African Americans who declared in the 1960s, "black is beautiful." At the same time, racaille has retained its stigmatizing power, as was seen in the fall of 2005, when rioting in the banlieues was fueled by anger over the use of that word by the then interior minister (now president) Nicolas Sarkozy to describe disruptive youths there.

7. Michèle Tribalat, *Faire France: Une enquête sur les immigrés et leurs enfants* (Paris: La Découverte, 1995), 174–82.

8. Fadela Amara and Sylvia Zappi, *Ni putes ni soumises* (Paris: La Découverte, 2003). The organization was an offshoot of the Fédération Nationale des Maisons des Potes, a federation of associations working for improved conditions in the banlieues. The first major initiative of Ni putes ni soumises was a nationwide *Marche des femmes des quartiers pour l'égalité et contre les ghettoes* (March of banlieue women for equality and against ghettoes) early in 2003.

9. See Laurent Mucchielli, *Le scandale des "tournantes": Dérives médiatiques, contre-enquête sociologique* (Paris: La Découverte, 2005), 85–107.

10. See Chérifa Benabdessadok, "Ni putes ni soumises: De la marche à l'université d'automne," *Hommes et migrations*, no. 1248 (March-April 2004): 64–74.

11. On the construction of media images of the tournantes and the catalytic role of Bellil's book in this process, see Mucchielli, *Le scandale des "tournantes"*, 11–32.

12. Alec G. Hargreaves, "Testimony, Co-Authorship and Dispossession among Women of Maghrebi Origin in France," *Research in African Literatures* 37, no. 1 (Spring 2006): 42–54.

13. Josée Stoquart, preface to Samira Bellil, *Dans l'enfer des tournantes, avec le soutien et la collaboration de Josée Stoquart* (Paris: Denoël, 2002), 12–13.

14. Mucchielli, *Le scandale des "tournantes"*, 19–22.

15. Mucchielli, *Le scandale des "tournantes"*, 33–84. Mucchielli's empirically documented findings parallel the specific cases described in Bellil's narrative: while the precise ethnic origins of her assailants are unclear, their victims—of whom Bellil was only one—were certainly of diverse origins, including several women of European appearance.

To Hell and Back

1. Jaïd and K.

"Thank you, girls. Take care, now."

The salesman with the big moustache hadn't a clue. He didn't see our checks were forged, he didn't see the fear in our eyes. Didn't see a thing. Unreal.

My girlfriend Sofia and I couldn't stop dreaming of those mega-expensive Westons, so we each swiped a check from our mothers' checkbooks and copied their signatures with carbon paper.

We just wanted to play in the big kids' league, be the kind of girls who wear Westons. I chose dark red golf oxfords and Sophia chose black slip-ons. Talk about burning money, let me tell you, we burned it up!

We flew out of that store carrying our old shoes inside big bags emblazoned with gold lettering, just flying from the rush of it!

Then we split up at the Gare-du-Nord. In the train on the way to Garges, I couldn't stop staring at my shoes, couldn't peel my eyes off them. Unreal!

When I got to Garges, I went to see Rachida and the others, so I could strut around in my brand new pumps. It was like riding on a cushion of air. Man, was I looking good!

Toward midnight, after hanging with the girls a bit, I decided to head home. I'd gotten in the habit of going home by passing through a part of the projects called *la Cité bleu*, to see the gang at the entrance there. You couldn't miss them. Come rain, come snow, come wind, they were always there. That night, there was Li'l Ball, Freezpea, Salim the Shrimp, Krazy Karim, and Schnozzface— the whole crew of "King Jaïd's" goons.

Jaïd was the hottest in the whole neighborhood, the one you respected and feared. His slightest wishes were orders. Yet I wasn't scared of him and his homeboys, I thought they were nice. What I took for friendship was actually vice; what I took for respect was nothing but lies. Because in reality, I was nothing but Jaïd's meuf. But that night, I didn't yet know it.

I was thirteen when I met Jaïd at la Cité bleu. It was summer vacation, and I was grounded. I had just been kicked out of Saint Rosary, a private Catholic junior high school. After being thrown out of two other junior highs, my parents had thought it wise to rein me in. It actually calmed me down a bit at first, at least in terms of whom I hung with, the daddy's boys who had had a kind of hold on me. I stopped going out and cutting classes, but I still wasn't hitting the books any better. I'd been a complete space cadet for too long already! School did nothing for me, and neither did those boys. So my parents decided to punish me by grounding me for the entire vacation. There was no way, however, that I was going to spend the whole summer watching sunbeams bounce through my bedroom window! Soon as I had a chance, I took off for an hour, three or four days, or longer, depending. I came home to wash up, change clothes, sleep, wolf down something, and get my ass kicked, and then I was off again. After my stay with the Catholics, I had reunited with old friends and fallen back into old ways: chilling with the girls.

That summer, I had gone over to la Cité bleu several times and Jaïd had begun to take a shine to me. . . . As I was new, the whole crew kept showing off in front of me. The question was: which of them would "hook" me? It turned out to be Jaïd.

I was thirteen, he was nineteen. . . . Jaïd was the blaze of the hood, dark-skinned, shaved head, eyes so black they should have scared me. With a body like Bruce Lee thanks to Thai boxing, which enabled him to wreck a fair amount of heads around him. As our relationship developed, I saw the fear and respect he inspired and the influence he had over the gang and the whole neighborhood. At the time it all made a big impression on me. Today, I'd run.

I fell straight into his trap, into the web he wove around me. I let his talk and his hot looks intoxicate me. At thirteen you believe in lightning bolts from heaven, you believe in love. It's the age when the wildest films go through your head! I was living in my bubble, in my dreamworld, and this bubble was also my protection against the blows I took along the way. Only Jaïd mattered. In his arms I sought the love I didn't find at home.

My troubles had begun when I turned eleven. Before I became a teen rebel, I was a little girl who loved art. I had started by learning how to read music at the conservatory in order to study piano later. I took classical and modern jazz dance. I was also interested in painting and theater. You might have called me a budding artist, but not a little bandit yet, believe me!

3

On the streets I became what we call a little caillera. I started to behave like a smartass, to pull cheap tricks with anyone, to go to Euromarché and steal the big craze at the time — granola bars and Burlington socks! In a word, I was always looking for a cheap thrill.

Before Jaïd I went out with boys to look good, to look old, to be able to say that I'd dated a guy. Stupid shit. But I wasn't in love. With Jaïd it was different. For me, it was serious. I was happy being looked at, being asked for, being "loved." I thought I was irresistible in his eyes and respected by the others. So-called friends fed this fantasy and I was consumed with pride. At thirteen being blond or brunette doesn't matter to boys; the important thing is having a "cute little ass."

Jaïd! I melted like an ice cube in front of him. It was all too beautiful for me. A big guy in the neighborhood, so handsome, so respected, interested in a kid my age, I couldn't believe it! He had a girlfriend, in fact, but that didn't stop him from shooting the shit with me and even doing the "I'm gonna hook you right in front of my girlfriend" routine! Today, I know how wrong I was. I tell myself that if I hadn't been so young and love struck, if I had been smarter, I would have seen the warning signs. But I was already numbed by life and I was too much in need of affection to be able to see anything at all. He played nice with me, and like an idiot I sucked it up! I believed in love at first sight, stuff like "He dropped everything the minute he saw me, even his ho." In the hood I became "Jaïd's meuf." Like there's "the king's noblemen," well, I was "Jaïd's meuf," his main girl, and that title changed my life. People looked up to me, they respected me, I felt important. And I might as well admit it: all that attention went straight to my little head.

It was my eyes that first drew Jaïd, and then the fact that I hadn't yet caught the "ghetto poison." It's true, even if I did stupid stuff, the "do it to them before they do it to you" ethos hadn't infected me yet. I was straight out of my Catholic school, I didn't live in the projects, but in a small private apartment block, and that was enough to make me the "little rich girl." I changed a lot in his company, I got tougher, but he didn't push me to steal, I had already done that before him and I would do it after him. Mostly, I just wanted to impress him, to be like him: a real hard-ass, feared and respected. A little kamikaze who didn't give a shit about anything, who had balls. Pursuing my relationship with him meant fighting the prejudices and taboos of completely outdated traditions and twisted minds. I was caught in a crossfire. Everything was jumbled up in my head and I didn't know where the truth lay anymore. I felt pulled between what my family background arbitrarily laid out as expected of me and my own dreams of freedom. I dreamed of being free. I didn't want to live in submission nor locked up at home, like the girls I saw around me. I wanted the same freedom a boy had — to breathe, to bite into life — what could be more natural?

I didn't realize that our relationship was twisted. I didn't understand that I was Jaïd's meuf without really being one. We saw each other from time to time. He'd take me in a corner, or over to his place, and dump his wad. I was a puppet in his hands, I let him do whatever he wanted, and I accepted it in the name of love, because no one had ever defined that word for me.

Despite my feelings for him, he dragged me through the dirt, humiliated me, and dashed all my hopes and illusions. He did nothing to warn me even though he could see me changing, degrading myself, destroying myself, right before his eyes. He didn't say a word, he just used me, sullied me, whenever and wherever it suited him. If my life was going to hell, he sure didn't give a damn.

Little by little, people lost respect for me. I was tagged with a reputation as an easy lay thanks to Jaïd, who talked about our "squeezes" in detail to his gang. He betrayed me with no remorse and I just kept loving him, sad little dipshit that I was, never figuring what a fake he was or what he was saying behind my back. Everyone in the gang knew when I showed up that I was going to get screwed. You can bet they were thinking, "Why not screw her myself?"

From the moment I met Jaïd, I changed almost beyond recognition. For my guidance counselors, the social workers, and my parents, I went from being a difficult kid to being a hopeless case in the space of a year and a half, the time I spent with Jaïd.

Okay, now that the scene is set, I can come back to that never-to-be-forgotten day when I showed up in front of the gang with my killer shoes.

I was walking by, wearing my Westons: "Bitch, those are bad!" Having bolted so much, it had been a while since I'd been back home. That evening, I told myself I'd better not overdo things, better go home, perhaps a bit unwillingly, a bit late, but I would make it home.

The whole gang was there with Jaïd, hanging out by the entrance. Everyone took in my shoes, including Jaïd. He spoke to me, and my eyes saw only him.

"Hey there."

"Hey there."

"Got a smoke?" I handed him one. "Nice Westons!"

"Thanks."

"You comin'?"

With those two pathetic words, I was on cloud nine. Oh, I never asked for much! Forget affection, forget tenderness! He treated me like a dog, and I was in la-la land.

He told me to come and I went with him, like a zombie. He took me to his basement pad. It was a basement room fixed up with a couch that smelled of gas and mold. I learned later that I was just one of a bunch of girls he led there.

"They're something bad, your Westons, nice and petite too, real chic!"

I was a little nervous he'd steal them off me and resell them, but a guy doesn't do that to his meuf! Little did I know that what he was doing to me was a thousand times worse. . . .

He pulled me close. He kissed me. I was flying: first these pumps, now Jaïd. What a day! After he made "love" to me, or rather after he relieved himself, he said I could go.

I am so sad today to have been so blind then. I feel sullied and ashamed to have accepted such wretchedness. To let yourself be dragged into a dark basement stinking of gas and shit, onto a rotten sofa with a real son of a bitch. It was pitiful, it was sordid. And stupid idiot that I was, I thought he loved me and I was floating in the clouds.

When I came out of the basement, the gang was still at the entrance. One of them called out to me for a smoke, so I went over to give it to him. He went ballistic right in my face, inventing some bullshit to draw me closer. While I was trying to understand what he wanted from me, the others came toward us. I couldn't see Jaïd.

A fist landed in my face, completely out of the blue. I felt my cheek getting hot. I tried to fight back but I was too late, a kick in the back threw me to the ground. I had no idea what was happening. Ten minutes earlier we'd been joking around, now wild beasts were tearing me apart. I heard, "Shut your trap!" as seven or eight animals took turns smashing my head down. They each wanted me to give them a "treat." I was getting more and more nervous. I knew I was close to losing it, but I tried to hold up as long as I could, despite the punches and kicks coming from every direction. They landed on my legs, my back, my stomach, my face. I held on, I fought back, I defended myself with all my strength. All of a sudden I heard a voice make them stop. Was it Jaïd? No, to my total surprise, it was his buddy, his best friend K.

K. was a hunk, a mass of solid muscle with a capacity for savagery. He was huge, with a neck like a bull, bulging eyes, and enormous hands made for knocking people out. People said he was a real butcher, a psycho. He inspired terror and everyone avoided having anything to do with him. He was the champ in all categories of evil. He'd already killed someone with his fists and gotten away with it by pleading self-defense. One day I saw him force a guy to hit another guy, for no reason at all, by threatening to smash him if he didn't do it. K. had tried to flirt with me several times, to joke around, but I was so scared of him I slipped away each time. That night, after K. yelled, the punches stopped and my attackers let me go. I was saved! The nightmare was over. Full of gratitude, I thanked K.

That's when he walloped me. He picked me up by my hair, dragged me, and then told me to stop crying and follow him. "Scram," he told the others. They split. The more I cried, the more he hit me. My head was almost bashed in and I was barely conscious. Terrified, I did as he said. We reached the highway, him pulling me by my clothes to force me to follow him. I was scared to death, I begged him to leave me in peace, to let me go home. I talked to him, trying to reason with him, but my words didn't make a dent, it was as if he didn't even hear me. At one point I managed to extricate myself from his grip, I ran with all I had. I was completely crazed. I tried to stop a car. I yelled, I screamed that they had to help me but the cars zoomed past, paying no attention to me. Infuriated by my screams, K. hit me again, full force. His fist smashed into in my face, which literally floored me. I was crying from exhaustion, impotence, pain. My face was flooded with tears and blood. Without an ounce of pity for me, he continued to beat me until I had no strength to react, until I realized that the only way I'd have a chance of surviving was to follow him.

So I did as he said. I followed him, wobbling, exhausted from this unequal, pointless struggle. Along the way he stopped and pummeled me to keep me terrified and passive. He didn't say a word. Even while I was following him, I kept trying to find a way to escape. I felt like I didn't have any strength left though, my legs were numb with terror.

Fear can be unreal. It can make you lose all your defenses, your ability to run or breathe. It's like a total paralysis: your body and your soul are whipped out. No end of people were to tell me later: "If I'd been you, I would have. . . . There's always a way to fight back. . . . Surprise your attacker, kick him in the balls. . . ." How many times I've heard such murderous little phrases, filling me up with guilt, pitiless comments made by people who have never felt the grip of true fear.

Finally, we arrived at the entry of an apartment block, then climbed to the third floor. We stopped in front of a dark door: I had enough time to read the name on it. Then we went into an apartment. It was clean, decorated in a neutral style, beige tones, with a big brown wraparound sofa. There was a television, a VCR, wall-to-wall carpeting: it was simple and rather comfortable. K. knew that after the beating he'd given I wouldn't scream anymore, so he started to talk to me as if nothing had happened:

"So hey, those shoes of yours are really killer. You thirsty? You want something to eat or drink? I hear you been getting it off with Jaïd. . . ."

I had no clue what he was up to. I was in a total panic. What was he after? Why was he speaking to me so calmly after he had just beaten me up a few minutes ago? I sat on the sofa, petrified. While listening to him, I looked around everywhere. I tried to memorize everything, telling myself, "Look around, remember it all, you never know, if they question you some day, you might need this information. . . ."

I heard myself answering his questions. What was happening to me? How could I talk like that with him? The truth is, I just faked it, I was too scared of getting hit again. The conversation we had gave me the horrible impression that I was going along with it, but what else could I do if I didn't want to die? Later, this thought would torture me for years. I felt guilty for appearing willing. But that day I knew I had no choice. I was trying to save my skin.

"Go clean yourself up. The shower's over there. And wash it real good down there," he told me, throwing me a towel. He watched me while I washed myself, to see if I did exactly as he had told me to do. I kept quiet, but I was fuming. Son of a bitch, asshole! He took me for a filthy pig. Listen, jerk, even when I was on the street, I always managed to stay clean!

I got out of the shower. He told me to come close to him. He went over to the VCR, put in a video. It was porn. "You scope and you do the same." I did it. I did everything he told me to do. I felt like vomiting, but I held it back. I was scared of getting hit again. I acted "nice" to get it done as quickly as possible and go home.

While I was performing to his orders like a robot, I used all my strength to shelter myself inside my head. I had it running a thousand miles an hour. I understood right away that it was the only place I had left. The only place I could escape to. He might have my body, but he didn't have my mind. My mind was mine alone.

So I imagined my parents, my sisters sleeping. I thought of everything in my life. And then I saw that name on the door again. I hung onto it. I called up more images: my friend Sofia, school, vacations in Belgium, Mama Josette, etc. Everything I could think of. Anything to keep from feeling that panting, that smell, that skin. Nor was there any way I was going to think for a single second about what he was doing to me. I didn't want any piece of that reality, and by forcing myself further into my mind, I managed to dissociate myself from what my body was "experiencing." It was no longer mine.

At last it was over. I couldn't say how long it went on. Now I was hoping I could leave, but instead he took me into a bedroom at the end of the hallway. The room was covered with posters and red lights. He told me to lie on the bed and he locked the door. Lying in the dark, I waited, not knowing what was going to happen. I lay there with my eyes open. My heart beat so loud it filled my chest and the whole bedroom. I was completely terrified. I thought he was going to kill me.

I heard a noise. A door closed. Then I heard murmurs. The bedroom door opened; another guy came in with K. I didn't know him. He was small, hairy, and much less stocky than K. He didn't say a word. K. did the talking. "You let him do what he wants. Don't get stupid, okay? Just be nice!" And then it started all over again. K. forced me to do stuff with his buddy.

I couldn't keep doing those filthy things. It twisted my guts, it turned my stomach and my heart. So I closed my eyes tight. I did what I was told, robotlike. I didn't resist, I became a kind of slave, a piece of shit, a worthless thing in their hands. "You're not making me hard, you filthy bitch!" he screamed and made me remedy it. He stank and disgusted me. I felt nauseous. I wanted to get them out of me, to get out of myself. But I was scared that the beating might start again at any moment so I did as I was told, consumed by fear and hatred. I begged God to save me, I begged him with all my heart and despair. My prayer rose from my guts, from my soul, exploding in my head.

But after awhile a third guy appeared in the room. I had never seen that one either. He asked the other guy to hurry up and, scoping the whole scene, started to masturbate. Then he wanted to force me to "do things" to both of them at once. I panicked,

I cracked, I started sobbing. I started to scream again, I begged them to leave me alone. K., who had left, came back in the room asking what was happening. When they explained, he threw the second one out, "Get outta here, you had your turn!" I found myself alone with the third one. I was as low as a human could get. . . . I felt like a piece of putty, totally spent, damaged, soiled.

Little by little, I locked myself in a black hole, a deep void. Nothing touched me anymore. It was like my mind had left my body. It wasn't me anymore there, lying on the bed, smothered by those hands, that skin, those smells, that filth, and that savagery, it was just my body, which had become an inert object, completely numb. The process continued and intensified: I had tried so hard to flee into my thoughts in order to extract myself from what was happening to me, that now nothing at all touched me. I was cut off from my body, I was anesthetized. I was somewhere else. It was like my body didn't belong to me anymore. Could it be dead? In any case those grave robbers, those vultures wouldn't have my soul; I found refuge and survived in my soul.

They did as they wanted with me all night long, giving free rein to their lowest instincts. I was even submitted to physical torture by K., about which I will not speak; humiliation has its limits. Reawakening these memories is a pain I accept only in order to bear witness. In the early morning only K. and I were left in the apartment, the others had left. Then K. went through another metamorphosis and I could barely recognize him. Again, he acted as if nothing had happened: he fixed me breakfast, he shined my Westons. "You see," he seemed to say, "I'm not a son of a bitch!" And after that he let me go.

I emerged outside, feeling like I had just arrived from another planet. I walked up to the bus stop like a robot. There I was with my torn sweater and my shiny Westons, miserable. My legs could barely hold me up. "Hurry up bus!" I didn't even know what my face looked like, I tried to read it off the looks of people nearby: they saw nothing. It was early morning, a new day was beginning for them, a day like any other day, and there I was. I had just stepped out of a nightmare. I tried to pass myself off in front of them as the-girl-taking-the-bus-like-normal.

I was gulping down a flood of tears. I stuffed back my sobs as far down my throat as possible. I felt a tight wad in my stomach, a ball of screams, of hurling fists, of swear words and tears. The ball was swirling with violence, poised to explode, to shatter into pieces. But nothing happened. There I stood, waiting for that damn bus. When it came, the driver gave me shit about the ticket and I screamed at him to leave me in frigging peace.

Now where was I to go? Home? I wanted to take off, go as far away as possible, so that no one would ever find me again, somewhere where they wouldn't ask any questions, where I'd be free, where I'd be safe.

2. Alone

I decided to go my girlfriend Sofia's place. I got off at the town hall and looked at the big clock on the wall. It was six o'clock in the morning, too early to go up to her apartment. I went into her building and waited in the lobby for an hour. I sat down in the stairway, my body anesthetized but not my head. It was turning at full speed, heating up, blaring with questions and thoughts. Nothing coherent, since I was in a state of shock. I badly needed to talk to someone.

"Bitch, Sofia, get up!" I could hear families waking up, going to the toilet, quieting their dogs, the bickering and fuss of morning routines. Each time someone came down the stairs I ran to hide. I didn't want anyone to see me in this mess. Why had I landed there? Who knew anymore? I had to talk to someone, quick, or else my head would burst. I did my best to climb the stairs. I was in luck. Sofia opened the door and she was alone.

"What's happened?"

"I gotta talk!"

She led me to her room, where I flopped onto the bed. I closed my eyes and didn't want to open them for a long, long time. Sofia was always a chatterbox, couldn't help but gab, so she started in on my shoes: "So, you loving your Oxfords?" I was at the breaking point, but I couldn't help trying to act again like nothing had happened. I got up and looked out the window, answering her without letting her see my face. "Yeah, they hated me at Garges! Couldn't talk about anything but! Serious!" And then I blurted it out:

"Saw K."

"No way!"

Sofia understood immediately what that meant. She knew about the reputation of K. and that gang. "Don't tell me! He screwed you, didn't he? He screwed you!" I showed her my bloody ear, my broken lip, the bruises on my body. Sofia stood silent, but not for long: "That son of a bitch! Son of a bitch! His mother's a whore! That motherfucker's going to hell!" She was in shock and stayed quiet for a moment.

"So, what are you gonna do now?"

"Dunno."

"You should go home."

"He's gonna kill me, Sofia, my father's gonna kill me!"

"You can crash here for a while, but you can't stay long."

I told her everything, reading the horror in her eyes. It blew her away. She had never dreamed this could happen to one of her friends. And just yesterday she had left me at the Gare-du-Nord, crazy about my shoes. Today she saw me standing there, a pitiful wreck. Sofia knew all about K's rep, about him screwing meufs. One day he had said to her, "You're on my list, one of these days I'm going to screw you easy."

"You've got to go home," she insisted.

"I'll go home, but first I need to chill a while."

When I got back home a little while later, no one was there. Phew! No explaining to do! Silence reigned in the house, but I felt only half protected there. The only security I had were the four walls. I feared a new terror. I imagined my father's blood-filled eyes, his jaw stiffening in rage, his fists ready to pummel me. When I imagined his reaction, I felt like a stray dog people throw stones at to chase away.

I'd received beatings before, but this one I really didn't want. No one was supposed to find out. "If you open your trap, I'll waste your whole family!" K. had told me as I left. I knew he was capable of it. I pictured the house on fire, my parents and my sisters fleeing in panic. All because of me. I must never say a word.

I took off my shoes and went to draw a bath for myself. A hot, scalding bath. God, did I need heat! I wanted to numb myself in the hot water, to dissolve into it. I closed my eyes. It was all turning, turning. . . . I dunked my head underwater. If only it could wipe away my memories as well, clean all this filth out of me!

When the water cooled, I emptied the bath and washed myself under the shower. I scraped away like a madwoman. I dug at my own skin despite the pain left from the attack. I wanted to get rid of every trace of the previous day. I soaped up three times, ten times, especially down below where I still seemed to smell it. I spent more than an hour cleaning myself. Good, I still had time before my parents got home, to get dressed, eat a little, lie down, and then split. I didn't have the strength to face their looks after what had happened that night.

I went off tormented. I didn't want to think anymore, just deaden myself. My only refuge. I had nowhere else to go. No one could take me in, no one could defend me against those sons of bitches. I was going to deaden myself to everything. On the way to the RER my heart was in my socks. In the train, I looked around everywhere, terrified of bumping into K. or his gang.

I was in such shock that I didn't even realize how dangerous it was to take the frigging RER. I went to see Rachida in Garges. She was my best friend, my sister in trouble, the first girl I had ever completely trusted. She shined like the sun. She had small, mischievous eyes, with hair like a Tahitian princess. I called her from outside so she'd go to the window and come down. We went up the stairs, to number ten. I spilt my guts. She cried with me, consoled me, comforted me a little.

"What are you gonna do?"

"Who knows?"

"You can stay here, my parents are in Morocco. I'm looking after the place with my brothers and sisters."

I much preferred staying with Rachida than going home. I felt safe at her place, even though I wasn't. I didn't go out for three days, just a little in the stairwell to have a smoke.

I looked up to Rachida a lot. She taught me how to hit clothing stores and how to drive a motor scooter. The first times I ever went clubbing were with her. It was with her that I first started seriously bumming around, that I got myself a little rep! We looked a lot alike. People often took us for sisters and that made us laugh.

At her place I tried to just get on with life, to act like nothing had happened. I went into Paris with her, I went out at night. I avoided staying at Garges during the day. When I returned home in the evening with her, I felt that fear in my gut again. Terrified of bumping into K. or the gang, I looked in every direction, using my eyes like radar to convince myself that the coast was clear. But then Rachida's brother started grilling me, unfortunately, so there was no way I could stay there any longer. I had to go home.

So, one afternoon, I returned, knowing there'd be no one there and that I could relax. At my parents' I was only comfortable when they weren't home. Then, alone, I could enjoy the silence. Otherwise, I spent my time cocking my ear, listening for what they were saying about me. Depending on the tone of voice, the intonations, I could tell if they were speaking about me or not. Sometimes I snuck into the hallway to listen. When the tone rose, I knew I'd be the one to pay.

That afternoon I settled into my little sister's room. I was safe there, strangely enough, because when my littlest sister was next to me, my father didn't dare touch me. He did do it once, but she went into such a tantrum he never tried it again. Half awake, I waited for the time to pass and someone to return. My father arrived first with my two sisters. I could feel he wanted to cream me because I hadn't been home for so long, but my sisters' presence prevented him. They were really happy to see me. They didn't leave my side the whole evening, sensing the tension and the danger it represented for me. So there I was, sitting next to them, next to my father, with my painful secret weighing upon me at every moment. Sitting at home with my mouth sown shut by fear, shame, and guilt. No, I wouldn't say a word.

Then Rachida told me "everyone" knew about it and they all knew I hadn't filed a complaint. I met assholes who asked me, "So, K. got you, huh?" smirking, as if they were saying, "Hey, got a smoke?" or "Dig that fat chick!" Each time it was like an electrical jolt. Images and memories flashed up that I struggled to forget. It was like a huge wave had swept across me and destroyed my reputation. To everyone, I had become an "easy lay." If I hadn't laid charges, it was because I'd wanted it. It was an excuse for everyone to criticize me and say aloud what they already thought of me deep down. A girl who "hangs around" is a whore, so she shouldn't complain when shit happens.

I felt trapped, unable to talk about what had happened. So I forced myself to not think about it and I kept bumming around with Rachida. I made sure I avoided certain places, certain gangs who wanted to get their kicks with me. When a girl gets screwed, all the guys want a piece of her. It's the law of the projects. A dangerous game started to unfold. I played cat and mouse everywhere, on the RER, on the bus, in the streets. My nerves were fried, I needed some air, I had to find a way to escape. Too much hate, too much incomprehension. Too much obsessive fear.

About a week later I managed to convince my mother to let me leave for Belgium. That's where the host family lived with whom I'd spent the first five years of my life when my mother couldn't take care of me herself. I kept quiet there too. They wouldn't have understood me anyway—there was such a gap between how I was with them and my life in Paris. It would have been too painful to explain how I lived in Paris. I didn't want to worry or disappoint them. So I kept acting like nothing had happened. What else could I do? I spent the whole of August with them. I took advantage of it, savoring each minute with them. It was the right thing to do, because those would be the last such moments in a very long time. I wouldn't see them again for ten years.

When I returned home, everything was the same: the same hitting, the same screaming, the same fury in my father's eyes, his brutality, his disregard. I went back to my habits with Rachida, without letting her know what was on my mind, the constant fear I felt. As for the others, I tried to get them to believe that what was being said on the street was a lie. I was out there cracking jokes, not crying in some corner. Seemed to be sufficient proof to me. Why couldn't I let my suffering out back then? I needed to so much. But I didn't have anyone to confide in or anyone to protect me. My heart weighed a ton and my head was out of control.

3. K.

One night in September, after my return from Belgium, I was in
Garges with Rachida and two other girlfriends, Nora and Soria.
We were just hanging out, shooting the shit, chilling. Eventually,
we decided to go to a club in Pontoise. It was girls' night and we
had a bit of cash for drinks. Rachida decided not come along finally, so the three of us took off. The club was a dump, but it was
one less evening at home for me and one more chance to numb
out. We were broke when we finally left. We waited for the train
at the Gare-du-Nord.

The late hour made us giddy and we were laughing about every little thing. The train arrived. We were laughing and pushing

each other as we looked around for a place to sit. The train was packed. People were on their way to work while we were on our way home to sleep. Just as we were about to sit down, one of the girls screamed, "K.!" The smile on my face froze. My heart jumped. I had to get out of there pronto. But K. had heard us, he was sitting just behind me. I started to run but in my panic I fell on the floor. He grabbed me, laughing.

"Oh, yeah? Trying to get away? Hey, sit with me a minute, let's do a little business, just the two of us!"

"Please don't! Please leave me alone! I never told anyone!"

He silenced me with a slap. It was a slap that threw me back a whole month to that sordid night I wanted to forget. He twisted my arm to make me move forward. "Oh, dear, have your friends taken off?" It was true, they had disappeared, without even pulling the emergency alarm. He forced me to sit facing him. He looked me up and down.

"You been to a club?"

"Yes."

"Where?"

"Pontoise."

"Who was that with you?"

"Nora and Soria."

"Rachida wasn't with you?"

"Please let me go!" I called out to the other passengers, "Help me! Please!"

"Shut the fuck up!"

He hit me several times. People just looked on, terrified. "What the fuck you looking at? She's my meuf, we're having a little fight," he screamed at those looking at him with seeming disapproval, yet nobody reacted, no one intervened. I was getting my face bashed in on the RER, and no one lifted a finger. I pleaded with people to pull the emergency alarm, but not one of them acted.

"So, Rachida isn't here. Doesn't matter. You're here. You're gonna get off at Sarcelles with me."

"Let me go, I have to get off here!"

"Oh, yeah? You don't get it, do you?"

And bam! He kicked me in the shins. People looked busily out the windows. A little farther up, there was a guy I knew, people called him Snake. I stared at him so he'd understand I needed help. Uncomprehending, he looked away.

When I saw the train go by my stop, I knew there was no more hope. I went quiet. I stopped pleading. Getting off the train at Sarcelles, I made a last attempt. Gathering all my courage, I pulled myself away from him and ran as fast as I could. K. was strong and caught me in a flash. He punched me in the head over and over, leveling me. "Man, you're dreamin'! This ain't no joke! Move your ass!"

He took me to a building he seemed to know. He got a key out and opened the door to the cellar, which was honeycombed with corridors. We went down one and he pushed me to make me go forward. We ended up in the trash room. Large green dumpsters, bags of rotting garbage strewn on the floor, and water running from a faucet. It stunk. If I had breathed in, I'd have puked. Memories of the last time flooded my mind. Fear, hate, and impotence shattered me. I remembered the impact of his punches, the force he was capable of putting into them. He flung his arm at me, landing me on the floor, and ordered:

"Kneel down. Here! Blow me!" I did what he said. "Take your panties off, you clean? Go on, go on, lie down!" I lay down like a robot. I knew that tune. I didn't resist anymore. The contact of my skin on the floor was disgusting. It was cold, it was wet, it stunk. I felt the floor turn my back to ice, but I felt nothing of him. I was inert, gone from my body. Like the last time, I escaped from it all, from him, deep into my mind. It didn't last that long this time:

ten, fifteen minutes, a half hour, forty-five minutes. I don't know anymore, but not the whole night.

"Didja like it?"

". . ."

"Answer me!"

"Yeah! Yeah!"

Asshole, asking me if I liked it! You make me want to puke! I'd like to spit in your face and scratch your eyes out! That's the kind of answer I wanted to give you, you bastard! I put my underwear back on, my thighs were all sticky. I felt filthy. I felt defiled. There was only one thing in my mind: get the hell out of that basement, get away for good. Leaving the building, we arrived onto a street lined with stores.

"You hungry?"

"No, thanks."

And there he went again, talking to me as if nothing had happened. We walked toward the RER station, ten, fifteen minutes, then he handed me a ten-franc coin and said: "OK, scram!" The coin burned my fingers. I threw it in the gutter and started running toward the station, crying. I found my friends there. They were scared. They had shut themselves up in the toilets. They couldn't pull the alarm. . . . Yeah. . . . Yeah. . . . I didn't listen to their excuses. I was thinking of what to do now, where on earth to go. The girls left me there, they had to get home. . . . Oh, you bet, for any kind of stupid shit, the girls were there! But now that I was in deep shit, there was no one.

Rachida was the only friend I had left, so I went to see her to tell her what had happened. She was cold and distant. She told me her brother didn't want to see me anymore showing up at their door. I couldn't believe it, I felt dead. She was abandoning me as well. For her I had risked my skin every day. And I had paid for her so she wouldn't have to. She was the one K. had wanted in the train

23

that morning. I couldn't understand anything anymore. What had happened to our friendship, the secrets we'd shared? We'd been like sisters, what had happened to her? The only thing I understood was that nobody truly loved me. People I thought were friends looked on coldly as each episode in my downfall unfolded, as if we had never known each other.

Returning home, I threw my clothes in the trash. I took a shower. I wanted to stay in it forever and didn't get out until the water turned cold. I put on clean pajamas and waited for life at home to resume its course: my parents returning from work, my sisters returning from school. I wanted to be a little girl in her pretty, fresh clean pajamas waiting for her parents to come home. That night, the warmth I longed for never came. No one ever did anything but chew me up and spit me out.

4. "Cellar Sluts"

Rap, graffiti, and break dancing had just hit the streets and it was giving us all a head trip. The projects were teeming with B-boys and potential fly girls, pumped up in their 501 Levi's, size 56, and those impossible-to-find high-tops — which you somehow managed to get your hands on and knocked everyone out with!

When I turned thirteen, the cool thing was to join a gang, to give yourself an American name and act like an American. The "game" consisted of pulling the stupidest stunts imaginable in order to make everyone think you were really insane. The wilder the gang, the greater its fame. Some gangs had more than fifty dudes. The best known were the Black Panthers, the Black Dragons, the

B-boys, the Warriors, and the BSP (The Pitiless Barbarians). The most notorious, because the most feared, were the Vicious Sharks and their little brothers, the Junior Sharks. Things were happening all over, people were squatting, at Châtelet, at La Défense, at the Gare-du-Nord. All these places had become dangerous hangouts where anything went when it came to showing how tough you were: fist fights, extortion, assaults.

Us girls also moved in gangs, mostly in "Panama," the old parts of Paris. We'd stroll around looking for a stool to fork us some cash for McDo's or take us out to a club, those of us who were allowed out at night. Either that or we'd steal. For us, it was a constant headache getting clothes, smokes, bar covers. Good-bye granola bars, hello MasterCards! There was also a constant hide-and-seek with the guys from the gangs. The hunt was on and you had to make sure you didn't get caught. I thought I was protected because I was going out at the time with Jaïd.

The gang phenomenon spread terror and shattered lives, among the boys as well as the girls. Among the boys, it was hardcore and pitiless, ending in either prison or death. As for the girls, no one said it at the time, but their fate was no more enviable. They fell prey to the gangs and suffered their violence in shame and silence. The common thing was to "screw" or "turn meufs." It was easy for boys: a shove here, a slap there, a bit of pressure, and the deal was done. A girl was shared like a CD or a sweater. They made her "turn" like a joint in what they called tournantes. They got animals to participate, all kinds of objects were used to spice it up. They'd take photos, and guys would "bust their sides" looking and talking about them. Girls were merchandise, they still are. No one is surprised anymore by tournantes, they've become the norm. The violence of what happens in the basements and in the trash rooms, or elsewhere, has only gotten worse since my time. Gang rapes are now commonplace, and the perpetrators are getting younger and younger.

The victims are naïve young girls, like me, ripe as plums. Girls who fall terribly in love with a little hoodlum, like I did with Jaïd, and who, because of that, end up with a reputation of being "easy," "a cellar slut." In the housing projects and hoods, the machismo traditionally found at home has come out onto the street. It now rules the projects. Boys and girls don't mix. Friendships and flirting can barely exist. On one side, you have the boys standing idle, passing their days "holding up the walls," as we say. There's a lot of deal making, joking, and banter down at the foot of the towers.

As for girls, there are two kinds: "good" girls and sluts. "Good" girls stay at home, do housework, take care of their brothers and sisters, and leave their home only to go to school. They've got "big brother" or "stay at home" written all over them and they're respected for this. The only way these girls can emancipate themselves is through education, running away from home, or lying. Then there are the others: those who hang around outside like boys, the cailleras. The ones like me who do what's forbidden, wearing makeup, going to clubs, and smoking. There is nothing wrong with this, but it's enough to make a rep for being "easy," for being a "cellar slut," for being a little whore. You can do anything to those girls because they have "no big brother" or "go out" or "hang out" written all over them. They're also called "she-rats" or "cum dumpsters" or "slop pigs." A reputation is very important in the projects. It follows you everywhere. It sticks to your skin. Maybe it seems like a cliché, but it really can be as make-or-break as that.

That's what I lived, that's how I was treated. For me, it was psychological torture to be treated as less than nothing, like a whore, a gob of spit, a piece of shit. It made me feel like I had no existence, like I was dead.

But in the projects no one is surprised by anything. Even the girls, who are the easiest targets, don't even react anymore to the violence, even the verbal kind, used against them. Insults, teasing about their physical appearance or style of clothes, getting spit at, getting slapped here and there, are all part of their everyday experiences. This kind of girl-boy relation has become an everyday power trip. The codes, prejudices, and attitudes to respect or avoid are legion. They even determine what you wear. A feminine girl in our neighborhoods is a slut while a girl in jeans and sneakers is a "good" girl. This kind of characterization is already a form of violence and yet it bothers no one.

As for the "cellar sluts," the little love birds, after being treated like shit, after being humiliated, abused, and dragged pitilessly through the mud by the entire hood, they then have to face threats from gangs if they've filed a complaint against them. Threats of burning down their homes, of odious vengeance, sometimes murder. But the worst is that the rapists consider themselves victims, "heroes" who complain because they get sent behind bars, because someone "sold them out." Nevertheless, if you asked them what they would do if a guy raped their little sister, they would all answer without hesitation: "I'd waste him!" Doesn't this logic make you want to bang your head against a wall?

Lots of girls, whom I knew at that time and who, like me, had their childhoods wrecked by a rape and its aftermath — bad reps, total rejection, and abandonment — "turned bad." Some are in prison, others are walking the streets, in psychiatric hospitals, or stoned off their asses. I often wonder how they survive. What's become of them? How can they manage alone, without anyone to listen to their distress, without an outstretched hand, an understanding smile? How can they make it out with no psychological support?

5. Two Families

My immigrant parents are very westernized, and yet their early upbringing left its mark on them. The way they were treated was the
only way to act: you force someone to understand by smacking,
punching, and kicking them in the butt until they really get it into
their heads! I am the fruit of two traditions, two totally contradictory ways of life. My parents gave me a traditional upbringing,
which no one ever explained to me except by beating, scolding,
and spitting. I also received a more European education, during
my early childhood in Belgium, from the host family where my
mother placed me. I stayed there for the first five years of my life;
then, when my mother took me back, I returned every school vaca-

tion until I was fourteen. In Belgium life was gentle and peaceful. Papa Jean and Mama Josette were very calm, well-meaning people who gave me their love and trust.

I was about a year old when I was welcomed by this young Flemish couple, who lived near Liege. Unable to have children themselves, they contacted an association called The Planters of Joy, who suggested fostering children of immigrants in difficulty. At first I was to stay three months, the length of a summer vacation. In the end I stayed five years. . . . When I think of my "love parents," a feeling of warmth rushes through me. I see the yard again, that amazing green countryside, the fields of corn. I recall the happy parties, and especially the silly things my "cousin" John did. I recall Christmases when Jean and I would decorate the tree. Mama Josette made hot chocolate, and then we'd go see Santa Claus who gave us all candy.

We'd go off fishing for frogs along the little paths above the village. We'd have fun poking around at the animals. It was a healthy, normal life, close to nature. My foster family was made up of attentive, affectionate parents full of love. Papa Jean was classy, and his love of life filled the house. He was calm and reflective, never a yell, never a gesture of annoyance. If I did something wrong, he helped me understand why I was wrong, encouraging my intelligence and listening with interest to what I had to say. It was eons away from the kicks in the face I later received!

Mama Josette was a real mother, though she could never have any children of her own. She knew what to do when I had a headache, she knew how to console me when I was sad, she was always giving me what I needed. She had those gestures, those words, that attentiveness. She was really interested in my life. I'll never forget her caresses on Sunday mornings when I'd go to wake them both up. She wanted a child and accepted me as I was, believing I was there to stay forever. When I think of those years, I still feel within me a big white wonderful light that warms my heart. If I had stayed with them, I never would have become the Beurette of the banlieue, the little tramp who sunk herself in hassles and misfortune. Who would I have been?

My real parents belong to a generation of immigrants, caught between the attractions of freedom promised by France and the desire not to forget their roots. My mother lost her father very young and only met her mother when she was six, like me. She spent her childhood in the Kasbah of Algiers, raised by my great-grandmother. When her mother took her back, her life was not all roses. She had six brothers and sisters and my grandmother was extremely authoritarian, particularly with her. She had to take care of all the housework: caring for her brothers and sisters, doing all the shopping, taking care of all the papers to fill out. She was subjected to unbelievable brutality, carried out by an uncle on the orders of her mother. This uncle once had the occasion to discipline me for talking in the street one night. He made me sit on a chair and tied my arms behind me. Then he began to slap me as hard as he could. Finally, he dunked my head into a bathtub full of water. That was nothing, however, next to what he did to my mother.

She grew up in violence, lacking the least bit of love. She suffered a lot, yet she has a heart as warm as the sun. When she was sixteen, she ran away from home to make her own life and moved to southern France, to Bandol. Although she didn't go to school much, my mother grasps things quickly and surely. She's a fast learner. She's got other capacities as well: she's determined and she knows how to fight. She met my father early on in France. He was a stud, an Arab version of Paul Newman. My uncle, always the same, learned about their relationship, searched everywhere for her, and sent her back to the village, where she had to stay a few months before she could escape again.

She was twenty-four when I was born, in Algiers, at the Hôpi-

31

tal Mustapha. My parents' lives were unsettled and full of hassles. They had to play hide-and-seek between Paris, Bandol, and Algiers. That's why I was born in Algiers. I don't know much about my father. Not a big talker. He was born back home also, in Bab el-Oued, a working-class neighborhood of Algiers. He was the runt of the family and he lost his mom very young. His father remarried with a real bitch who practically martyred him. She beat him raw, didn't give him food or shoes, and kept him from going to school. His older brother, who got the same treatment, also beat him. His childhood was a horror, and his suffering made him later unable to show any signs of affection. When he became a teenager, he ran away from home, it was during the war, he smuggled arms and was tortured before coming to France. He arrived in Paris with false papers and managed to live like that for a few years. That's when he met my mother. My father was a caillera, a small-time punk. He did some dumb stuff and took five years. It was the end of the Algerian War and the courts were heavy-handed when it came to prison terms incurred by Algerians.

My mother found herself alone at twenty-four with me to raise and her husband in prison. To keep my father in France, she had to have work, own a home, and show a stable income. She worked herself to the bone, sometimes holding several jobs at once. She worked on main line trains and slept at the terminal cities. She worked hard. She had to place me in foster care in various corners of France and told me stories of how she sometimes found me in a filthy state, starved or covered in bruises. One memory of my early childhood remains engraved in my mind. My mother had gotten me all ready, I smelled nice. I had put on my favorite dress and I was all content. I can remember a place with doors everywhere and long corridors. There was a small, windowless booth painted cream color. I was on my mother's lap. In front of me, there was a window and in the middle of it a circle of holes. It was the speakerphone.

My father was in prison and I was in the visiting booth. I did not understand why I couldn't go sit on his lap and give him a kiss.

It was during this time that my mother heard about the Planters of Joy, and that is how I went off to Papa Jean and Mama Josette's home. After meeting them my mother knew she could have total confidence in leaving me with them. It was a wrenching separation, but what other choice did she have? During the five years that I stayed in Belgium, my mother slaved away at shit jobs in order to take me back and create a home with my father when his prison time was up. When I turned five, she wanted to reclaim me and get me started in school in France because I spoke only Flemish.

I have a clear memory of that. I see myself crying, bawling even. I am in the hall of a sad, gray building. There are broken mailboxes, strong odors of a musty basement, and lots of garbage. Four people surround me, I am in the arms of a woman, and two arms pull me from her embrace. I scream, I do not want to go with that lady. That lady was my mother. That was the end of the happy life I had been leading, walking in the fields with cousin John, playing with the animals. That was the end of the tender world where I had blossomed as a child.

Fortunately, I returned there every vacation. Whole trainloads of us immigrant children would leave for Belgium, Holland, or Germany. We had little pink or orange cards attached around our necks that indicated our destination. We were scrubbed spotless. I remember thick socks and polished shoes. I remember colorful outfits, frilly dresses straight from our "benefactor," the cheapo discount store Tati, of which our moms were particularly fond.

No one ever explained this turn of events. I had lived in Belgium five years, then I was returned, like a package. No one ever spoke to me about the years my father spent in prison, although they marked me for life. I imagined fifty thousand different accounts, probably none of them true. At home not a word was said. There was simply

33

a fait accompli, as if I had no right to know what had decided my fate. My parents must have reasoned that the less I knew the better. I could feel this dark secret pulsing in everything around me.

So that is how I came back to my "true" parents. They lived in a banlieue, the Parisian suburb of Saint-Denis. A dreary apartment with dreary parents. Money problems, quarrels, a total lack of communication. A whole other world, and a cruel awakening after my early childhood in paradise. My status changed when my first sister was born. At nine, I became the oldest child with everything that implied in terms of obligations, in other words supporting my mother with the housework and babysitting my little sister. It was too heavy a burden for me. I did what I could to please them, but it was never enough, especially for my mother, who never stopped repeating all day long: "When I was your age, I did a thousand times more work!" When I turned eleven, my second sister was born. It was also the age when I became a "young lady," as they say so prudishly where we come from, and when I started more and more to rebel against this education in submission. A lot of things had changed, in particular the weight of authority at home had become overbearing. As a result, I started staying away from home. I stopped getting back on time, I stopped going to classes regularly, I forgot to pick up my sisters at day care or at school; as they say, I just did "whatever I pleased."

Getting bawled out, beaten, insulted for any small thing—none of it had any effect on me anymore. So they ended up forbidding me everything: my clothes, my wall posters, my records, a girlfriend here, a night out there, music classes, dancing. The only thing left to distract me was the street. Perhaps I could have been a well-behaved child if I had been spoken to instead of beaten. Instead, it was the street that opened its arms to me. I started to skip classes, to hang out, to steal, to run off more and more often.

I didn't belong in the street either. I was considered a little rich girl because I'd been to a private school and came from a middle-class home. Both my parents were working and there was no big brother to watch over me. So I didn't match the typical "Beur" model, with tattooed, wrinkled parents and a bunch of brothers standing guard over me. Out in the street, I didn't become a little punk overnight, I didn't wake up one day telling myself, "That's it! Today I'm feeling like Grandizer, I'm nuking everything!" No, not at all. Before reaching that stage I got a lot of things thrown in my face. A simple look would get me "done in," the "You-fucking-said-I-said-what?" kind of mess. Fights would be triggered by a wrong word here or there, and in those situations there were always people close by, ready to feed the flames with, "What! She said that!" A whole truckload of bastards and bitches benefited from my innocence. They fucked me over good. They had a blast doing it, the assholes. You had to stand up to it and I did: I gave as good as I got. I had no big brother to defend me, and in the end I didn't feel secure anywhere. There were pressures on me from all sides. How was I to understand what was being forced on me, an education in beatings and prohibitions, inequality between boys and girls, and stifling taboos, after the love I'd known with Papa Jean and Mama Josette?

6. The Charge

After the incident in the RER, I stopped going out. First of all, I felt cruelly wounded by the betrayal of my friends; second of all, I was scared to death of bumping into K. again and having to suffer the same torments over and over. I stayed locked in silence. I was scared, I was ashamed. I didn't say a thing but it was all I thought about. If I spoke out, I already knew what people would say: "You asked for it by hanging out on the streets." At home I was already considered a whore. To admit what was done to me would have been the same as admitting they were right. No way would I do that. But if I had stayed holed up at home any longer, I would have lost my mind.

I didn't have a choice for a time. School had started again a few days before and I had no school to go to. I'd been thrown out of three already. I had asked for a place in a sales-oriented vocational school, but no high school wanted me. I understood them, considering what was in my file. In two months my whole life had fallen apart. Everything had blown up in pieces. Yet I really didn't grasp that what had happened to me was a crime punishable by law. For me, those guys were just bastards who had had cruel fun with me. I was already so used to violence and bad treatment at home and on the street that I thought it was a fact of life. The desire for vengeance didn't even occur to me. Why was that? What had I done wrong? Why didn't I know how to do anything but blame myself?

I even thought I deserved what I was going through because I wasn't a virgin anymore. For Muslims, a girl losing her virginity is a sacrilege, and I knew my father could kill me for that. I had slept with Jaïd. On top of that, I was a runaway and a thief. I didn't listen to my parents or my teachers. . . . So I couldn't complain if I'd been raped. That's what was being said about me, but it was also what I thought about myself.

I couldn't stand staying at home anymore. I dreamed of drawing and painting, and I began to seek out something in that direction. Finally, I was given a chance in a professional high school of fine and theater arts, despite my delinquent-girl file. I was insanely happy. I put all the energy I had left into my studies. That school was my one chance, my only hope to make it out. I invested myself one hundred percent. I wanted to mend my ways and become like the others. I couldn't forget, however. Deep down, a small muffled voice tried to be heard. Its screams circled around in my stomach. It howled down there, it burned, it tied itself up in knots. I felt a ton of emotions jostling together and tearing each other up. But I put all my strength into keeping them quiet. Nothing got out. As for my head, it was boiling over, a constant commotion. I filled my brain with banalities to keep it spinning so fast it muffled the distress call of that small voice and stopped me from wasting my time on memories.

I guess I knew, deep down, that I wasn't strong enough to face that reality alone, that it would have killed me. So I denied it passionately, I acted as if it didn't exist. As if my body and my heart weren't suffering. My invisible shell protected me and allowed me to pull the damn wool over everyone's eyes: the teachers, the students, and especially my parents. My parents were the hardest. I pictured myself in the kitchen with my mother, split between the desire to find relief by telling her everything and the fear that terrified me. Not a single word ever slipped through my lips. I was paralyzed. Every night I scanned their faces, trying to guess whether or not they knew. A part of me wanted it to be known, I needed help so badly. The other part was too scared of the consequences. If my parents found out that I was not a virgin anymore and that I had been raped, it would have only ended with insults and blows. And then, how would the gangs have reacted, Jaïd and especially K.? I felt like a pinball tilted by others to every which side.

At school all went well. I liked what I was doing. The teachers were cool. It was a totally other world. Suddenly, my understanding of school changed and my attitude shifted. I stopped skipping classes, I got there on time, and I behaved myself. I didn't want anybody to know anything, to blow my chances. And besides, I was with students who were so different from those I had known! It wasn't *Beverly Hills* but the people there were polite and respectful. What a change! The boys and girls mixed in a natural way like in a real high school. My class was full of budding artists who all looked cool, a bit hippy. I was happy to learn new things: art history, drawing. I had come into that high school with a rotten file, accusations, disciplinary recommendations. The guidance counselor had warned me, "If you're late once or mess up once, I'll throw you out!" I couldn't have been happier. I had succeeded in getting accepted despite my reputation and, what's more, into an art school—my dream! Bet your butt I slaved!

November came around, a Wednesday afternoon. My sisters were at the rec center. I was in my room, my father was in the living room. He wasn't working that day. I heard a knock at the front door. I got up to open it. It was Rose, Sofia's big sister, accompanied by two girls I didn't know. I panicked: my father didn't allow girlfriends at home or even on the phone. "Look, we found out what happened to you with K. and we want to ask you to press charges with us, because he assaulted us too." Their names were Pauline and Clarisse, and they had been attacked a day apart by K. at the train station in Sarcelles. Pauline had obviously heard about my story from Sofia. She was twenty, she had a job, she was a grown woman, not a girl like me. And she had tons of energy. She tried to convince me to press charges. "You can't let that bastard go free! He only tried to paw me but I'm pressing charges! With what he did to you, he should go to prison." I was in a panic, my head was spinning, I had no idea what to do. I was so scared of my father, my legs shook. That was when the living room door was flung open. "What the hell is going on here? You, back to your room!" Pauline was the first to speak: "We'd like to talk to you, sir. It's about your daughter." My father threw a furious glance at me: "Get to your room!"

Then he invited the girls into the living room. I was in my room trying desperately to hear what I could. I heard nothing. I opened the door silently and glided into the hallway to listen better. A waste of time, they were speaking too softly. I went back to my room and waited. I heard him get up in the slippers he shuffled around in all day long. He was coming toward my room. I pretended to be studying. He threw the door open, his face full of spite, and came toward me. "Move it!" When my father speaks, it's like an earthquake, my whole being gets swept along, tossed around, shaken up. He throws all his contempt and brutality at your face and it hits hard! He doesn't necessarily yell, he can play you coldly, it's terrifying, and you freeze on the spot. I stood there in front of him and the other girls, terrified, awaiting the fateful question.

"Is it true what your friends are saying?"

"Yes."

Phew, it was a relief to say "yes." Now my father would take me in his arms, he'd protect me, he'd say, "Who is that bastard who hurt my little girl? Don't you worry, I'll make sure he gets what he deserves, your father's here, you don't have anything to fear now. Everything is over, I'm here, I'll take care of you. How do you feel, my little girl?" Instead, there was no hug; he just howled, "Get back in your room!"

Relief? What relief? I still felt scared to death. I waited to see what would happen next. How would my father react? Very oddly, he didn't hit me. He called my mother at work and spoke to her in Arabic so I couldn't understand a word. Later, I learned that Pauline had persuaded him to press charges.

We went to the Pontoise police station to file our complaints. Pauline was there, her mother, Clarisse, and I. Neither my father nor my mother thought it necessary to accompany me. So I had to face this new challenge alone. We were received by several officers who took our depositions separately. The cops tried to persuade us to drop charges:

"C'mon, girls, you sure it's not because he ditched you, you're not trying to get back at him, are you?"

"NO!!!"

I had to repeat my deposition several times, describing the agony over and over, with cops who were constantly coming and going. One was eating his sandwich, another asked in front of me, "Which case is this?" And then there were the questions like, "How long did that blow job last? What did he tell you? What did you do to him? You're sure about what you're saying?"

I had no medical certificate, no bruises to prove what I was saying. It was just my word against his. Only two people had seen me after the rape: Sofia and Rachida. Sofia didn't have a telephone, but Rachida did. I gave Rachida's number to the woman officer. She called and came back assuring me Rachida would come to give a deposition. Not only would Rachida never come, but she would also warn the gang of my charges. She flaked out on me, she protected herself. She had chosen her side. She chose to resign herself to what was being done to girls. She chose to not think, she chose betrayal.

It took me years to get over her betrayal. I wanted to smash her face in and I swore I would someday. Years later I met her in the street. She didn't recognize me. "Shit, what do I do, tear her to pieces? . . ." And then I watched her very closely. Rachida had become a junkie. She was sad to look at. I had known her so pretty, so young and bright. She was less than zero, totally blown out, half dead. Life had taken revenge for me. So I went on my way.

I could see that my story intrigued the cops. What? A girl gets raped two times and doesn't say anything? I tried to explain to them that the gang's threats had terrified me, that I had wanted to protect my family, and for that reason I had stayed as quiet as possible. I didn't feel well, sitting in front of that lieutenant and his colleagues. I felt dirty and humiliated a third time. Their questions and doubts threw me back to my guilt. All those people coming in and out, those looks, those questions made me feel guilty. I was guilty of disobeying my parents. They were quick to remind me of that. Cops are real psychologists! I was guilty of running away. Guilty of being raped. And to top it off, guilty of not saying anything.

I began to regret pressing charges. The cops didn't understand. They couldn't imagine what the guys in those gangs were capable of, which people were only just starting to talk about. The cops only knew about small-time gangs. They hadn't a clue about what was happening in the basements of the projects.

I had been at the police station for a good while. It was night outside. It must have been eight or nine o'clock. I was still in the lieutenant's office, waiting. I assumed they were busy checking out our stories to see if they matched up. A lieutenant returning from patrol entered the office. "Why are you here?" I was confused. Where should I start? Tell the whole story over again? I sat there speechless. He left and called a colleague. After a long while, he came back and showed me a picture. "Is that K.?" I looked at the photo. Even in a photo his head terrified me. My legs let go. I shook and fell back in my chair. Just don't show anything, no tears.

"Yes, that's him, those bulging eyes."

"Well, what do you know! I've been trying to catch that one for a while!"

Then he took out a picture of Jaïd.

"And this one, know him too?"

"Yeah, he was my boyfriend."

"Did he do anything to you?"

"Nope."

Only today, in writing this book, do I realize that Jaïd was far from innocent in my story. He drew me into a veritable ambush. For years I believed that, since he wasn't present at the time of the rape, he was innocent. And then, feeling guilty for having slept with him, I didn't allow myself to criticize him. I could have pressed charges for nonassistance to a person in danger and accessory to rape. Neither did I press charges against those in the gang who were there that night, because the beating they gave me was nothing compared to what K. and his two accomplices did. I also forgot about those two girls who were with me in the train and who abandoned me without calling for help. And most of all, I forgot about Rachida. I would have loved to press charges for betrayal, to attack her in court for the crime of betraying my trust. Was I too generous or too misinformed, I can't say exactly. What I know for sure is that even if they didn't care at the time, in the end, life did not spare them and justice was dealt in my favor.

"You sure he didn't do anything to you?" insisted the cop.

"I haven't gone out with him for a while now."

"But this guy is K.'s big buddy!"

"Maybe."

I went out to join the girls in the hallway. The cop showed them the picture. Clarisse broke down in tears, Pauline appeared stronger but also recognized him immediately. "We've been trying to nail him for a while. He's already up for a case of prostitution." I realized that I'd escaped pretty lightly.

Clarisse, at the time of the events, was nineteen years old, with a face like an angel and blond like a Swede. She was a student, a neighbor of Pauline. That particular night, she went out to see her boyfriend at Sarcelles. At the station, K. tried to pick her up. When she ignored him, he smacked her and tried to rip off her T-shirt. She managed to get away and take refuge in a store. K. took off. The next day, Pauline went to see her friend at Sarcelles. At the station, he tried to pull the same shit he did with Clarisse. But Pauline, who had done French boxing, knew how to defend herself.

"They both managed to escape, but not you?" I was asked. "You couldn't get away? Why didn't you try to defend yourself more? You wanted it, didn't you!" I let those filthy little words seep into my mind. They destroyed what little self-esteem I had left and piled more guilt onto the weight I was already carrying around. But it turned out that Pauline's testimony confirmed mine. It so happened that the day I was attacked in the train, Pauline was a floor below and heard my screams. She thought it was a couple having a fight. . . . The investigation was now launched.

A lieutenant accompanied me home, it was on his route. During the ride, he tried to get information on K. and Jaïd's scams. "I have no idea, all I know is what they did to me. That's enough for me!" It was eleven o'clock when I got back, my parents were watching TV. I was fried. The cops' questions had exhausted me. It was the same old tension at home. Not a word for me. Not a question about what I had gone through at the police station. Not a comforting word or look or bit of attention. I was alone amid a sea of indifference with that huge weight on my chest.

Later, my mother called the police station to learn about the proceedings. She never asked me one direct question about my psychological state, my feelings about events too dreadful for a fourteen-year-old kid to bear. As for my father, he never said a word. I'm past trying to understand why they didn't make that effort for me.

I found a plate of food awaiting me in the kitchen, like a dog his dish. I felt desperately alone in front of it. Rejected. Useless. Dirty. Guilty. I made myself real small, I made as little noise as possible. It was like I wasn't even home. I had never felt at home there, anyway. An invisible, mute speck. I felt my father's hostility hover in the air, his contempt, his fury. The silence hung there, making me feel sick. I ate my dish despite the ball lodged in my throat. I could feel it growing inside me, a ball that expanded malevolently. It would never leave me.

The next day, my mother woke me to go to school, as if nothing had happened. So I too tried to act as if nothing had happened. . . . On the way to school, I made up a million plans: I was going to fight it, I wouldn't let K. win. I'd be the stronger. I'd get my diploma, a nice job, a wonderful life, despite all the mess and the horrors I was living through. I clung to a senseless hope. I didn't allow myself an instant of doubt.

I didn't know then that I would have been right to complain, to cry, to scream. No, instead of that, I shriveled up, I made myself as small as possible. I didn't want to be a bother, I didn't dare look them in the eyes, broach the subject. I stayed in my room most of the time, afraid of confronting them. I only left to go to the bathroom, to drink, and to eat. The gap between us widened. My parents, from whom I had a right to expect understanding, protection, and love, closed their eyes to my despair. I was entitled to nothing. In front of me lay a void, a silence, a glacial contempt. They acted as if I didn't exist, as if nothing had happened. Slowly but surely I was dying from neglect.

7. Mathieu

Having pressed charges, another question now arose: should I have a lawyer? My parents discussed it without me, as usual, and my mother came into my room to tell me what had been decided. They always proceeded like this. The only time they chose to play psychological parents, the "I'm here to talk face-to-face" type, it ended with a gob of spit landing in my face—it was a cultural thing with us, the gob of spit—and the minute I opened my mouth to respond, I got yelled at or slapped.

So there my mother was, standing in my room, and I heard her say, "You know, we're not sure we can win . . . trying to get damages awarded, the lawyer . . . it all costs money." I was already not listening. I didn't care a bit about winning. It wasn't a damn horse race! Argh! Wake up! We're talking about guys who raped and tortured me, who humiliated me to the core, who have surely blown my life to bits, and you, you speak of damages?

It seemed to me that I would never be correctly defended, that my assailant would come out of this more or less unpunished, and that I had pressed charges for nothing, opened my mouth for nothing, and maybe even risked my life for nothing. If she thought, "we're not sure we can win," it was because she didn't trust me. Did she think I was maybe lying? I sensed that I myself had lost all trust in my parents, those people who judged me, held contempt for me, shut their mouths, their doors, even their hearts on me. . . .

Despite the cruelty of what I was experiencing, I stuck to school. At least there I had a steady framework. I continued play-acting, feigning to be carefree, nice, smiling all the time. But deep down, it was an open wound. At home I was now reproached for not having broken down. My mother thought I was abnormal to not be more affected than I was by what had happened. It was too much! She managed to make me feel guilty for that as well. I thought, "maybe I am inhuman, maybe I am an unfeeling monster." I still didn't realize that hiding my emotions was the only protection I had.

A little later, my mother talked to me about an association that defended the rights of children. Who had contacted her? No idea. In any case, it was free. I went to consult a lawyer in Colombes, Madame B. She had short, light brown hair, an austere face, and a husky voice. I placed great hopes in this meeting. Here was a person who defended the cause of children, someone who'd finally understand me! It started off badly, her first comment left me cold. "What do you want?" she asked in a perfectly indifferent tone. You'd have thought we were in a grocery store. "Two pounds of tomatoes!" I felt like answering.

Instead, I took it upon myself to explain the situation because my mother didn't know how to start. "Oh! How old are you?" She didn't even look up when she spoke. She sure possessed the art of putting someone at ease. . . . And to think I was expecting the attentiveness of a specialist, boy was I attended to! When I think that I was about to place my destiny in the hands of that woman! I could have screamed, "She's not the one I want! Fat pig!" "Fourteen," I answered her. She raised her head, looked at me, and said straight out, "A fourteen-year-old has no reason to be out at that hour!" And blah, blah, blah. . . . I knew that tune. She obviously believed I didn't blame myself enough. Bitch!

I held my tongue. I'd already stopped listening and wouldn't listen to her again. I sat through it, but I felt defeated. Suddenly, nothing mattered. I could feel myself dying a bit more. Another hope dashed. When I considered that she'd studied for years, that she defended sexually abused children, and that her comments didn't even rise above those of my parents, it killed me. The association she represented was very famous. There was even a big French actress who did their ads. It was an association that filed civil suits without taking on the legal defense of the child. After this meeting, I could no longer see their ad without feeling like puking. "Yes, yes, come help mistreated children. . . . Yes, yes, we have to speak out. . . . Yes, yes, we have lawyers who defend the rights of children!" Stop treating people like idiots! You thought it was enough to ask for money and give out a phone number to have a clear conscience? I sincerely believed those people would defend me, I put my trust and my life as a mistreated child into their hands. With what result? The rest of my story will show where it all led.

During this time I received news of the investigation. I learned that no one had yet put their hands on K., after a month and a half of searching. That meant I was very much exposed. I could run into him at any moment. There were countless anonymous phone calls. Sometimes they insulted me; sometimes they were silent. I was in a state of constant stress, which I bottled up along with everything else. The state of shock I was in left me paradoxically energetic for my "social life." I managed to hold on in school, for a while. Soon, however, I cracked. Too many risks when I was out. I was paranoid, I didn't trust anyone anymore. Moreover, it seemed like no one could do anything for me. The calls at home drove me nuts. Each time, they created an atmosphere of tension for which I was blamed. "You see the life you force us to lead with all your fooling around!" they bawled at me each time.

In my neighborhood I saw guys who weren't from here passing by, lurking around. I knew they were looking for me. When I passed by them, I looked away, I hid, I was scared. I had nowhere to escape. On one side there were these ferocious animals lurking around. On the other, the very people who were supposed to protect me, my family and the lawyer, pushed me a bit further under each day. My parents were killing me bit by bit with their daily, deadly little words full of innuendos, their reproaches, their disapproving looks. I wished I could have run far away, started a new life, a new identity. I dreamed of waving a magic wand over my rotten existence. In the meantime I escaped into daydreams full of tenderness, justice, and understanding.

Fortunately, I had high school. At least there I found a kindness that fortified me. The groundskeeper, the janitor, the cleaning women, the cook, and the nurse were my friends. The cook spoiled me in the kitchen, as did the nurse in the infirmary, where I often went for migraines. Each visit, she made me a hot chocolate and drew me into long conversations. I was like a stray dog, I had a terrible need for my little corner of affection, for my bowl of caresses. I was a beggar for love. I lacked it so much! What was

49

I not ready to do to receive attention, recognition, and affection! I was capable of anything. Of playing the sucker, the bimbo, the clown. I wanted to please, I wanted people to like me. To squelch this little voice in me that kept endlessly repeating what others said of me: "You're a slut, a little whore, a filthy punk."

It was Mathieu who finally noticed me. He was half-Vietnamese, half-Berber: a sexy combo. He had black, almond-shaped eyes and smooth, caramel-colored skin. He was a hippie type who loved the folksinger Renaud. Each time he saw me, he chanted, "My goddess, the one I love, my princess, the one I'm with." In his eyes, I was pretty, I was stunning, I was gorgeous. Finally! Someone loved me. He turned me onto books, helped me discover another world, one without violence or hate.

At first our eyes met in the hallways, the playground, the cafeteria. Then, little by little, he entered my circle of friends. Finally, one afternoon, after classes, he waited for me outside. He wanted to walk me part of the way. In the end we spent the whole afternoon together in a park, talking about literature, music, film. We talked about our future and remade the world. I remember it well because I knew I'd get in trouble when I returned home. Time flew.

After that afternoon, I wanted never to leave him, I wanted to stay with him for good. My craving for love pushed me into the arms of the first guy to show interest in me. I believed in it. They wrecked a lot of things in me, but not my capacity and faith in love. I remained a big love addict, in spite of everything.

Mathieu was gentle and very attentive. He made me laugh and forget. He stroked my hair, called me princess, and looked at me like I was a wonder of nature. In his arms I felt good and forgot everything. My life was split in two: during the day there was happiness with Mathieu. At night there was misery. The wounded animal that I'd become reappeared with my parents, along with obsessive thoughts and fears of threats, of K.

Mathieu had two or three close friends at school. The nicest was Pat, a big punk rocker with platinum blond hair, big boots, and chains all over. Pat went crazy over me. He made up a wild spoof of a comic strip with me as heroine. Then there was Feed Back, another friend. He was not that bad looking either. He had a Mohawk and his clothes were black like the singer in The Cure. Another nice guy, for sure. I'll never forget Pat and Feed. They brought the sun back into my miserable life and opened the doors wide for me. From time to time, we'd end up at Feed's place to share a snack and laughs. A nice little breather after classes.

One night we were all there, Mathieu, Feed, Pat, and me. We were cracking up, eating, listening to music. Out of nowhere I exploded. I said I was not going home anymore. That I was too scared to live any longer like I had been doing: constantly on my guard. I proceeded to tell my whole story. It left Mathieu in tears. Pat was silent. Feed offered to let me stay at his place, his father was never there and anyway, he was cool. It was late, Pat and Mathieu decided to go home. Mathieu promised to come by before class. I stayed at Feed's.

For the first three or four days I went to classes, but then I just stayed in the apartment, feeling no desire to go out, so great was my need to rest my mind. I felt good at Feed's place, he was super nice with me. Mathieu came every day to see me. Then one day he also decided to not go home anymore, to stay and support me. He didn't want to leave me again. He stopped going to classes too and we stayed all day listening to music, eating, sleeping, making out. We were crazy happy together. Pat came to see us every day, bringing news of school. They were beginning to wonder, "Where are Mathieu and Sam?" We decided to leave Feed's place because it was beginning to get worrisome.

Mathieu lived in Gagny and he had some friends there who

could put us up. People told him about Adeline, a funny plump little eighteen-year-old who looked like a huskier version of the actress Susan Sarandon. She was spoiled rotten, little Adeline. She lived in a huge house where her father had fixed up the cellar for her. It was as big as the rest of the house, made into a little apartment with all the amenities. A place you could die for! She found both of us "cute as pie" and agreed to put us up. It must be said my story shook her up. She wanted to help me. She had also taken in another guy, Pascal, who had failed to report for military service. It seemed he was screwing her in exchange for the roof she was offering. Adeline was in love with Pascal and spent her nights waiting for him. She regularly flipped out and I consoled her all day long. Pascal would come home from time to time and calm her under the sheets.

We started to have serious money problems. Pascal had a "brilliant" idea: breaking into houses. He and Mathieu formed a team. Every evening, they went fishing and brought back what they found: TV sets, videos, clothes, food. None of us could see where it was all heading. We had become discount "Bonnie and Clydes." Together with Adeline, we counted the resale cash. All this money galvanized Mathieu and me. We dreamed of moving to the south, of living like beach bums. We dreamed of giving everything that surrounded us a good kick in the butt, of starting fresh somewhere else. Mathieu swore he'd pay any price to see me happy. In the meantime I put bills aside for our plans, bills I would break the next day. . . .

8. Runaways

One night we were all together enjoying a nice calm moment. I was lying in Mathieu's arms, talking with Samir, a new pal. We were joking and cracking up, because we could hear Adeline and Pascal loudly making up between the sheets. The door bell rang. I tried to interrupt Adeline, but she was much too busy to be disturbed and told me to go get it myself. I hesitated because I was a runaway. But I went anyway and found myself standing in front of Mathieu's father. I could recognize Mathieu's Vietnamese traits. His dad was livid. He asked to speak to Adeline.

"That's me," I had the cheek to tell him.

"I'm looking for my son Mathieu, someone told me he'd be here, with a girl named Samira."

"Nope, don't know no Mathieu or Samira. And anyway, I don't have anyone living here. Who told you that?"

"That's none of your business. Look, is my son here with that other floozy or what? That's why he's here, you know, for her little ass. That's what draws him here, the little hussy! Let me in so I can see what's going on here!"

Bastard! How dare he insult me like that! It was like being hit in the teeth. What if Mathieu's father was right? What if I was nothing but a slut? I kept my cool so as to not make a mess of the situation. I couldn't let him enter the house at that moment, with Mathieu who was of course present, Adeline who was performing her somersaults, and me who wasn't Adeline. . . . The problem was that he wanted to come in. I blocked the door. "If that's the way it is, I'll come back with the police." Right then, Adeline, who had finally finished with her acrobatics, popped up.

"Who are you?" Mathieu's father demanded.

"Adeline, who else!"

I was in deep shit. I cast Adeline a wide-eyed look and blurted, "Actually, my name is Nora. Since Adeline was busy, I thought I'd stand in for her."

"What the hell is this crap?" screamed Mathieu's father who didn't believe a word.

"But it's true, sir, Samira is telling the truth!" cried Adeline who had just forgotten that my name was Nora.

"You dirty little liars! You've been messing with me from the start, I know Mathieu's in there. You can't gain anything by stalling, I'll come right back here with the cops. Then we'll see if you think this is funny! You little hussy, all of this is because of you! He wouldn't be here if it weren't for your ass, you—you—whore!"

Now he had really roasted me, so I took off the gloves: "Bastard! Asshole!" I flung my whole repertoire at him. It made him totally lose it. Now we were really up shit's creek!

Mathieu and I decided to leave. But where should we go? We hadn't a clue, but we left anyway. In a few minutes, we gathered our things and kissed Adeline goodbye. Right then, the door bell rang. Adeline went out into the back yard to look and informed us the cops were out front. Since we couldn't leave by the front, we left by the back yard. Our only escape route was across the roofs of three or four neighboring houses. Mathieu helped me climb up first. Once up there, I caught the bags he threw to me, then he joined me. We took off into the night, going from roof to roof, hugging our duffle bags to our sides. You'd have thought we'd been doing it all our lives.

"This leads to a back road, we'll take it and walk to the train stop at Chelles. OK?" I nodded silently and followed him like a little soldier on a commando raid. I trusted him completely. I'd have followed him to the ends of the earth. Our little Bonnie and Clyde hearts were beating a mile a minute. We took the train, arrived at the Gare-de-l'Est, dead tired and completely bewildered. Where should we go? What should we do? We clutched our dreams. We'd never split up, whatever they told us. We would leave together . . . and already we saw ourselves basking in the southern sun, the two of us staring out to sea.

Meanwhile, we counted our pennies. Not enough to go past Juvisy. All our savings had been spent on food, cigarettes, and weed for friends. We had just enough to buy a Double Whopper at the Gare-de-l'Est Quick. This situation couldn't last, but neither of us wanted to face the obvious. We weren't ready. We still believed in our plan. We wanted to believe in it with all our hearts.

We got back to Adeline's completely wasted with only one desire:

to sleep. Adeline nevertheless filled in the picture for us. Mathieu's father and the cops had come by. They found out that we weren't there and summoned Adeline to the police station the next day. We were all in deep shit. But we were too exhausted to think, the roof caper had worn us out. With our arms wrapped around each other tightly, we fell asleep like kittens.

About six thirty in the morning I heard a noise outside. I saw the shutter open and a hand break the windowpane. My scream woke Mathieu. I ran to hide in the shower. From there I heard a voice yell, "Where's my daughter?" It was my mother. She had managed to track me down. She tore through the house screaming and found me in the shower. I was struck by a powerful urge to laugh and when she pulled the curtain aside, I burst out in peals of laughter. I laughed so hard my stomach hurt, I couldn't stop, I was crying. It was my nerves, of course. Mathieu and Adeline didn't know whether to laugh or cry. Although pretty emotional, the situation sure did have something freakish about it. Man, can my mother get serious! To break a window to get into an apartment, turn the place inside out with such authority, you gotta have guts! She should have been a cop!

My mother knew she was walking on eggshells. She couldn't go too far if she wanted to take me home. I guess I didn't really have a choice though. Mathieu and I both had to go home. After hours of discussion, I left halfheartedly. I returned full of bitterness, because I had really believed in my romantic escape. I returned scared to death. My mother talked in my ear like a little songbird. "It's all going to change. . . . We'll be cool with you. . . . But, you know, you gotta do your part, you're not an easy child, you know. . . . Honest to God, when I think it over, I can't understand you. After what happened to you, you think you'd stay put. And there you go running away again and going out with another guy. You're not sick of guys after what happened?"

She understood nothing. She didn't understand that I was scared of K. and his gang carrying out their threats, attacking her and my father or my sisters. The only way to protect them and myself was to be elsewhere, far from home. My father, that evening, said little, just "I told you she was a slut!" That was his way of summing up my first taste of love.

My return to school was tough going. Everyone knew what had happened and I couldn't deny it. The other kids found our story very romantic and reacted warmly, even with admiration. As for the teachers, on the other hand, they gave us grief; we had missed more than a month of classes. They gave me a second chance though because everything that had happened to me was now public knowledge: the rape, the investigation, etc. But now, Mathieu started to give me the cold shoulder, which hurt me a lot. He started to tease me and even hit me. I had no clue what was happening, but I didn't let him get the better of me. There was no doubt he'd gotten a third-degree brain washing from his dad.

Suddenly it was done. The police had arrested K. and his two accomplices. But it didn't stop me feeling scared because people were still trying to intimidate me to get me to drop the charges. I was always bumping into guys or girls who told me I shouldn't have told on K. and his gang, and that I had better watch out for myself. Other times, guys who knew me shoved me or spit in my face. It became unbearable, to the point that I thought of stopping going out. I felt like a boxer who takes one punch after another without being able to lift himself up, take his breath, and punch back. I swallowed it. I did, however, talk to the cops about the threats, the calls, the aggressive encounters. They didn't take me seriously. They thought fear had made me paranoid and reassured me of their protection.

After K.'s arrest I was summoned to the police station in Pontoise. My mother could think of nothing better than to send me off with my father because, in her words, "it's a chance to get close." Interesting, huh? On the train ride to Pontoise I sat facing him. It was pure torture. The whole way there and back, not a word was said, he showed no interest in me except for a furious look. It was like I was headed to the slaughterhouse. I felt lost in a jumble of emotions. Words like "at fault," "dirty," took root in me and refused to let go. Added to that was the fear of what awaited me. Once at the police station, I was told they had arrested my three assailants and that I needed to identify them. I refused, no way on earth did I want to face them. I was told it would happen through a one-way mirror.

My father went with me but he had no idea what was up. He didn't know that there were three of them, three young men of color in their twenties. Neither did he know where it had happened. My folks hadn't shown much curiosity about the matter! I watched his reactions: his jaws tightened but not a word left his lips. I could sense that I disgusted him, that I had deeply and definitively disappointed him. I was ashamed of what he heard, and that increased my guilt tenfold. Oh! Thanks, mom, thanks for your great idea. . . . It was nuts to think this ordeal would make us closer!

I ended up in a darkened room with a little rectangle in the middle of the wall: the one-way mirror. Two cops accompanied me and told me to take my time, to look carefully, to say if I had the slightest doubt. As soon as he entered the room, on the other side, I recognized him. I recognized him despite the changes he had gone through. He had let his hair grow and his beard, but his look hadn't changed, he still terrified me just as much. My legs started to buckle. Then I recognized the other two, even mixed together in a group of cops. Even with the handcuffs and surrounded by cops, K. scared the shit out of me. I had the impression his gaze was fixed on me, despite the one-way mirror, and in his eyes I read all the harm he could inflict on me.

I made my depositions and then I was free to go home. What I had just experienced was doubly painful due to my father's presence. Another wound that festered deep within. That evening, at home, I heard my father talking with my mother in Arabic. His tone was nasty and hard. I couldn't bear the constant hostility anymore. So I shrunk back into myself even more, lying low in my room. I didn't want to believe that my parents could hurt me that much. It couldn't be real. They didn't see me, they didn't help me, they avoided me.

Today I can see that I modeled my behavior on theirs. At no moment did I pay serious attention to myself. I showed neither tenderness nor respect to myself. I spent my time judging and hating myself. I constantly fled from myself. Could I have done differently? No one had ever shown me I deserved better. How could I have felt anything positive about myself when my parents presented me with such a dark, filthy image of myself? I had entirely taken on the image they had of me.

9. The Grind

Since the police line-up, my father wasn't speaking to me, wasn't even hitting me, he didn't want to touch me again. I was too dirty in his eyes. I didn't understand why he had wanted to go with me.

It was the morning of January 7. I was in my room, drawing. My mother was at work, my sisters were at school. I was therefore alone at home with my father. Out of nowhere, the door flew open. Standing over me, ramrod straight, with his hand on the doorknob, was my father. He glared at me with a look full of hatred and bellowed:

"Get out, pack your bags! You disgust me, you make me sick! Get outta here now and don't come back!"

"..."

It took me a moment to grasp what had happened. I was dumbfounded. I was like those people who sight a flying saucer and wonder if they're dreaming. Had I heard right? Disgusted him? Made him sick? Are those really the words he had used? I couldn't believe it. With those few words, he had cracked my spirit, smashed me to pieces. He had waited to be alone at home with me to reveal his true thoughts! What an act of courage, father! There really is no shame in saying it, even if it is a blasphemy in our culture to criticize our parents: my father was a *tetrai*, a traitor. No bones about it.

As for the "get outta here," I was used to that. I had heard it all throughout my childhood. First, it was for my mother. When he was smashed, he would throw her out naked, with me in her arms. We'd spend the night at the police station or in shelters. Then he began to pick on me. He started to throw me out any time of night, in my nightgown, half naked. Meant nothing to him, as long as he was sleeping in his warm bed. He woke me with a kick to the stomach, screaming at me to get out, just like that, because he was after me for nothing, for some little thing I did wrong. It would usually happen on Fridays, his day off, his drinking day. It was his way of celebrating that holy day in our culture. The biggest paradox was when he kicked me out because I'd run away. Those days it was, "Go back where you've come from!"

If the memories weren't so awful, it might seem comical. I came to expect to be thrown out on Friday nights, it was almost a habit. I lost count of the number of times I slept in basements or staircases. And when it was too cold, to keep warm I walked all night. Usually, I struck a straight line from the suburb where I lived to the Porte de la Chapelle in Paris. It was a good ten kilometers. I did the round trip, all alone in the cold, walking all night long to keep warm, my hands sunk in my pockets for warmth. Sometimes I'd get back at dawn. Other times, I slept in the subway. I could sleep best on the Balard-Créteil line because it was the longest. Then I'd go see my mother at work. I'd get a hundred francs off her and leave again for the day. It became the norm. I was between eleven and fourteen years old. It was my life. I didn't ask questions. Sometimes I even left without anyone asking me to.

When I turned eleven, my parents started to forbid me to do things. I was no longer allowed to play outside, to have girl-friends and even less boyfriends, or to get calls at home. I wasn't allowed to do anything anymore, only homework. No one spoke to me about anything but school, household chores, and watching over my sisters. My mother hassled me. She was constantly on my case and made me redo the same thing five or six times because it wasn't done as she wanted. "Samira! Come here! Are you screwing with me or what? That's not how I taught you. Do it again right, I'm watching!" She could empty out a closet if I hadn't put things away the way she wanted. She'd talk at me till I was sick, showing me all the while and for the ninety-ninth time how it had to be done. To bug me, she'd binge talk. She'd re-proach me for everything, my attitude, my way of talking, even things I had done three weeks before. Everything got dragged in. She had a talent for rolling everything together and the energy of a crazy woman.

"At your age I didn't have your freedom, your clothes. The luck you have! My mother meant everything to me, not like you! I filled out all her paperwork, I helped her with everything. I never dared behave the way you do. You're nothing like your cousin Yasmina, she listens to her mother!" And on and on. For hours she'd go on, till I started to boil. When my father wasn't there I'd yell back, "I'm not your maid! I don't give a shit about my stupid cousin blah-blah, I'm me, ME! Stop comparing me to every-one. And what do I care about your life, it's not the one I wanna lead!" To make her leave me alone, I had to fight back harder and harder until she finally cracked. It was a dangerous, violent game of one-upmanship.

My mother would really have preferred to raise me as she had been raised back where she came from, the hard way. Back home in Algeria it's like that, girls take a beating without batting an eye. I know my mother had a hard life, that she was the victim of a culture where women are treated like dogs. I know she had neither love nor consideration nor the least affection. Still, I blame her for her silence. I blame her for letting my father inflict his violence on us. I blame her for not saying anything when he beat me or made me spend the night outdoors. Today, she can't remember—it's so convenient! I blame her for not fighting for me, for allowing my psychological degradation, for making no effort to understand me. I blame her for not making me the apple of her eye.

She made all kinds of excuses for my father and none for me. She asked me to be understanding with him, because he'd never been taught anything different. It's not a child's job to under-stand adults, and I was way too sunk in my suffering. All I could do was fight back against their form of child rearing, quick to hand out slaps and beatings instead of words, full of unspoken taboos and glaring injustice toward girls. To express my rebellion, all I could do was run away and act up. I grew up without the net that would have kept me from hurting myself and without a tutor to help me grow straight. I was an orphan. I had no at-tachments, no ties, no structure. I learned to make it on my own by hardening myself. I made myself what I was with whatever means were available, however I could.

Exasperated by the atmosphere of constant repression that reigned at home, I started to run away. The first time I ran away, when I was eleven, a friend took me in. My mother found me again after a week and she wanted to press charges against the friend's mother for corrupting a minor. I didn't want this lady to get in trouble, for she had sympathized with me and taken me in, so I returned home. My mother hammered away at me all the way home with her usual complaints about my behavior and I blew up.

"I don't want to go home! I can't take it anymore, living with that man who's always screaming and hitting me. I don't want him to ever touch me again!"

"OK, he won't touch you again. But you have to make an effort too!"

"No, I'm not the one who should make an effort. He should move out, he's driving me crazy!"

"Oh, so that's what you want, huh? You want to wreck my relationship with your father! You're nothing but a selfish pain in the butt. Who the hell do you think you are? You're not the one giving orders. C'mon now, you're going home!"

"Go fuck yourself! You just want me home to do the housework, that's all. Well, if you're just going to forbid me everything again, I'm not coming back."

Then, completely out of the blue, she took out a phial of tear gas and sprayed it in my face. I screamed with pain, but I still managed to give her a stiff kick in the shin. She then left me there and took off. I couldn't see a thing, my face was on fire. My eyes burned and the more I rubbed them, the worse they got. After a quarter hour I'd recovered a little and sought refuge at the friend's home I had just left. Her mother took very gentle care of me. She was outraged. I was embarrassed, deeply ashamed.

The next day, I heard about a person who helped young people. I went to see her. Her name was Edith. She was young, tall, brunette, with hair like Kim Wilde, a popular style then. She offered me a drink and I explained my troubles. She invited me to stay at her home that night, before finding another solution. While I waited, she drew a bath for me and offered me dinner. I felt good in her home, I could have stayed there forever. There were paintings and musical instruments all over the place. Edith was an artist and her friend a musician.

The next day, they both decided to go to the police station to file a complaint and to attest that I was living with them. They made an appointment with a juvenile judge and a social worker. While I waited for it to get worked out, I stayed with them. I felt good there. A judge heard my case and decided to immediately place me in a shelter. I ended up at Raincy. I was happy to be there, with "French" people as the phrase went. At least there, they spoke to me, I counted for something. I preferred being a DSS kid than a member of my own family. I felt safe, like I'd found a real haven. Finally, they'd leave me the hell alone.

I continued to go to junior high school, in seventh grade, but I didn't study. I had no head for it. The important thing was to be far away from home. Everything else was a joke. My mother wanted to get me back. She painted me as a difficult child, who rejected authority. She managed to hypnotize the judge with all her arguments. And she added that she did not live in the projects, that she had a job, that we were a respectable family, etc. . . . She took the air out of my tires, so to speak. My mother can be very cunning when she wants to be. . . . After six months, since all was quiet at my parents when I went there on weekends, the judge decided that I could return.

Once home, my parents blamed me for presenting them as abusive. My father didn't speak to me again for a long time. My mother made insidious reproaches and turned the situation on its head by making me responsible for everything. I felt misunderstood by the judge and by my parents.

It was from that moment on, what I call the Granola-bar period, that I began getting into trouble. I was almost thirteen. I skipped classes, I hung out with delinquents. I became rude, a big mouth, a real pain! Then I became a runaway and a repeat runaway. I took pleasure in annoying people in the bus, insulting them for no reason. I yelled, I showed off. I adopted the logic of gratuitous violence, the law of the fittest. If I didn't exist at home, outside I wouldn't be ignored. I was seen, I was heard. Actually, all I did was throw back the violence inflicted on me. Everything I'd packed inside came flying out. Then the one-upmanship really began, always more, always stronger. I charged like an angry bull, head down, ready to demolish anything in my path. I charged ahead like that for several years, unthinking, caught in an endless spiral.

Running away, re-running away, stealing, meeting Jaïd, keeping bad company at Sarcelles, the constant grind, the street. . . .

10. Shelter

Seventh of January in the morning. Here we go again: My father had just kicked me out because I "disgusted him." I cried packing my bag. I knew that this time, whatever happened, I wouldn't be coming back. I swore deep down. I promised myself that I would not return until I was eighteen years old. Whatever happened. I usually didn't keep my promises, but that one I did.

I was outside in the rain, the sky was as gray as the bottom of my heart. I was loaded like a mule. I'd taken everything: my clothes, my shoes, my drawing materials, with the big green folder that was a hassle when you walked in the subway. I had my books, my school stuff, everything. A real Bedouin of the projects! Where to? After the stuff with Mathieu, my mother had notified a judge about the danger I was in: the threats from K.'s friends and my father's hostility. I was given a place in a shelter in Nogent. On that occasion, my mother fulfilled her parental role. That's how she is: she can do the rottenest things and then the best. Of course, I would have preferred to see her defend me in front of my father and wished she'd said he was the one who should leave and not me, because he was the one who couldn't handle the situation anymore. But she didn't have enough courage to confront him in that way.

The problem was they wouldn't be ready for me at the shelter for another week. My father couldn't wait for me to find a roof over my head before he kicked me out. I called my mother at work, she told me to come to the store. She was working then in a clothing boutique in Saint-Germain-des-Prés. She could feel that I was determined to not return home. Another solution had to be found. She called the shelter, which agreed to take me a week in advance. An emergency case, as they called it.

I cried all the way to the shelter. I cried without knowing exactly why, but I sensed that something had changed for good. Nothing would be the same. My father's words came back to haunt me. I had put up with the insults, the beatings, but I could not forget the words he had used. His "disgust" shattered me, mortified me, dragged me through the dirt once more. No, I would never go back there.

At the shelter, Jean-Pierre, a social worker and assistant director, received me and gave me a tour around the premises. I had a room with a key and a view over a quiet backyard. Quiet as the suburb of Nogent-sur-Marne with its trees, its riverside promenades in summertime, its faded colors in winter. There I was, standing in my room, a bit sad around the edges. Before I could settle in, I sat on the bed and broke down in sobs. I couldn't put words to what I was living through. I was just living through it, that was all. Afterward, I went to have lunch, putting on my dime-store smile for that first meal with the others. On the menu: steak and French fries, my favorite. Jean-Pierre introduced me to the others. Martin, Li, Salima, Clarisse, Gérald, Patrick. I put on a happy face full of self-confidence. I was used to being confronted with harsh situations and I knew well how to mask my feelings. I smiled all the time, not letting up for a moment so no one was encouraged to ask me questions about the reason for my arrival. Since art school, my appearance had changed: for a while I swapped my gym shoes-and-sweats outfit for a somewhat more eccentric look, definitely cooler. But the gym shoes-sweats-bomber jacket outfit would soon come back.

I had no intention of being a pushover in this shelter, and it was Martin who was the first to know it. I can't remember what it was we fell out about: a cigarette or one word too many in my direction, I'm not sure. What I do know is that his ninety kilos didn't scare me and that I got into a huge fight with him. This shut everyone up. After that, I earned some well-deserved respect. I entered into the shelter system, got my unlimited subway card, my hundred and fifty francs, and my four movie tickets a month. Cool. After our rather muscular introductions, Martin became my big friend. He respected me because I quieted him down. He came each night into my room to tell me about his day. He was a real nice guy but suffered like me from never being loved at home. In the shelter he was a big mouth, but I always defended him because he was a bit thick in the head. There was also Gérald, from La Courneuve. I knew one of his friends. At first, he wanted to test me, see if I was an "easy" one. It's the same everywhere, they always look for a way to maneuver. It's only when they see that they have no chance at all that they respect you. I was experienced by then, I didn't let them take advantage of me. I didn't have to use force anymore. For example, I managed to maneuver two girls, Clarisse and Salima, into stealing for me the things I needed. It's like that in shelters: naked vice. Gérald also respected me for that.

I understood what behavior was necessary to gain respect, it wasn't in my nature but I was good at it. I acted the hard, pitiless loudmouth. I attacked first so others would back off and leave me in peace. I understood that you have to treat others like you don't want to be treated yourself. Nevertheless, I knew about cultivating a pleasing, cheerful side. I dangled the carrot gently. I juggled my emotions, but hid my deepest feelings. One evening, I was called outside. I went out and saw everyone huddled together in the back of the yard.

"You smoke?"

"Of course!" Little girl that I was, I thought they were talking about cigarettes.

"Come have a drag!" I didn't want to pass for a dead beat, so I took three or four drags on the joint.

"Where you from?"

"Sarcelles."

"Oh, yeah? Pretty tough place!"

"Yeah, whatever."

Obviously, the joint was just an excuse to find out where I came from, who I was, etc. I had no desire to gab, I concentrated on the weed's effect. I felt funny, but no question about showing it. I kept a tight hold on myself. The joint turned and came back to me. I took another three or four drags.

"Hey, don't hog it!"

"Relax! I'm giving it back to you."

Then I went back up to my room. I lay down on my bed. My head was spinning wildly the minute I closed my eyes. I felt like vomiting and yet I liked it at the same time. I liked it because I felt like I was flying, free from it all. I took off from reality and it made me forget my whole messed-up life. I flew, I turned pir-ouettes, leaping over my bed like an astronaut in a weightlessness chamber. Was this weed? Shit, I was hooked!

After that episode, every time there was a joint circulating I was there. Then I started to deal and steal. I had to struggle with my first joints, which looked more like hard candy than real joints. Sharing didn't come easy to me, I always bummed off the others, making them think my pockets were empty. From time to time, I took out a joint to calm people down.

My main worry at the shelter was to make people respect me, by being cunning and most of all by not showing my feelings. Neither to the young people who shared my life, nor to the social workers who lent me support. I always said that everything was fine. The shelter did offer me a steady framework, with rules for living and a solid structure. I enjoyed personal consideration that I would never have received at home. Even if it was not ideal, I could remake my life there for better or worse.

The important thing was to be far away from my parents. When I thought of them, I was disgusted by my mother's atti-tude. I really had the impression she had chosen my father over me. She had abandoned me to his authority without considering my pain, she had closed her eyes on the unacceptable. I wanted to mark an X over such parents. After a while, my mother started calling me to see if everything was going OK. My mother was like, "Get out, you stink. . . . Come back!" She was a total contradic-tion and I grew up surrounded by those contradictions every day. She tried to corner me and buy me back. She gave me money, showered me with gifts, ignored the joints. What was she after? Maybe she wanted to buy herself back, clear her conscience? Or maybe she wanted to prove to the social workers that she was a good mother and that I was being unjust with her? My mother was no fool! Each time I complained about her to others, she would do some good mother thing, all generous and kind. Later, she'd try it with my shrink, but she wouldn't find much meat there. She'd get sent packing with no words lost.

But my mother was especially resourceful when it came to discovering where I was. That's how it was one day when I hadn't returned for a few days, she managed to discover where I was hanging out. I must have been twelve or thirteen at the time and I was sitting out in front of a school. My mother went bonkers that day. She arrested me. She jumped out of a car, took out her half-price subway card as if it were a police badge, flashed it around at the kids there who could only think the worst, and yelled, "Police!" She grabbed me, threw me on the ground, put handcuffs on my wrists, and threw me into the car. And just like that, the car took off, with my aunt at the wheel! The shame I felt! In front of all my friends! Soon as I got in the car I got the slap of my life. I still wonder where she came up with those handcuffs. My mother is a regular one-woman "Starsky and Hutch"! If she had only put that energy into resisting my father . . .

I wondered why she always wanted to get me back, since she never seemed to think of changing anything. She continued to ignore the hellish tension permeating our home and seemed to completely deny the horror I'd been through. Was it too hard for her? How could she have not understood my disarray in suffering all those events or felt my loneliness and my feelings of rejection? How could she have not sympathized with my suffering? Even for two seconds put herself in my place? Couldn't she see that on top of all I'd suffered, I'd had to deal with all the consequences: the threats, the name-calling, the police interrogations, my father's disgust and brutality, everyone's looks and taunting rejections?

No one was going to figure me out at the shelter either. I didn't act like a girl who'd been raped. I hadn't shrunk back into myself with the traumatic air of a victim. To the contrary, I was bursting with life, nonchalant. I took up a lot of space and I had a strong influence on the others. So, for them, I didn't have problems. I respected the hours, I returned on time. The system offered me enough freedom, so I didn't abuse it.

However, I continued to keep silent. I didn't want to let anyone in on my story, I felt horribly ashamed and guilty! Or the person had to have the magic key: words that drew me out and softened me up, and a heart to understand me. In the absence of that, I closed up, I blocked all emotionality. I froze my heart because I didn't have an ounce of trust left in those around me and I didn't want to suffer anymore. I was scared of being betrayed, misunderstood like I'd always been, by my lawyer, my parents, my girlfriends. I was taken for a delinquent, a street punk, a hard ass, a slut, when I was just a child in difficulty. The social workers criticized me for my tantrums and didn't hear them as cries of distress. I closed the mouth of the little girl bawling inside me. I shushed her up because she was given no right nor place to cry. I barricaded myself, like I was a strongbox made of reinforced concrete.

I went wild when attacked. I stayed on guard, I observed, ready to pounce on those who wanted to take advantage of me. I would not be taken advantage of anymore, I had paid too steep a price for being nice and sweet. The rapes had changed me from top to bottom, they repainted my worldview in black. Even if my home life before had been hard, I had still felt life itself was good, and I liked people.

A person cannot remain buried in reinforced concrete. The violence and distress haunting me had to explode. My body found a solution. Bodies are so smart! Mine started to have epileptic seizures. Not just anything, mind you! My strength grew ten times stronger, and I sometimes needed seven or eight people to hold me down. I howled like a wounded animal, my body reared up, convulsed. A huge electrical discharge released my suffering and my rage. After the seizure my body was broken, completely spent, but I felt better. I retained no memory of what triggered the episode, what I remembered was all the attention I got that time.

So my seizures became a new mode of expression. At the height of them, I spewed up everything I held back. The pressure of my blocked emotions was released and everyone finally took care of me. And even if everyone saw me as a sick person, everyone saw me. That's what was crucial for me. That little wave of attention filled my heart. How monstrously pathetic!

One day, I had a seizure at the high school. I was dragged on a stretcher across the schoolyard and driven to a hospital. The stupid doctor there gave me Lexomil. I took the pills for a while, but they left me comatose. During class, I couldn't dot an i, I was putty, I actually felt asleep. I felt like a drug addict, like I was completely wasted. I disliked "nerve" pills, and anyway, my nerves were not what was sick, it was my heart. I had a relative who had been treated with that horse remedy; he'd gone completely bonkers. I had no desire to resemble him one day. I knew in my gut this shit was bad for me.

I don't like doctors who automatically prescribe Gardenal, Temesta, or Lexomil to people in distress. They swallow a dose, fall asleep, and drown their troubles with this shit, but their suffering is still there. It's a vicious circle: since the cause of your malaise is not treated, you keep taking more! For fear of resembling that relative, I put a quick end to that madness.

I did what others wanted for me, I made them happy by submitting to the round of scanners, EKGs, tests of all sorts designed to track down my "illness." They told me I probably had something in the brain that triggered the seizures. The docs concocted some pretty wild scenarios. But no one ever took a look at the psychological aspect of my seizures. One doctor even exclaimed, "Listen, you cannot have such violent seizures so frequently without being a good actress!"

"Well, well, well, doctor, you've found me out. After all these years, I admit I'm the best actress around."

At the shelter I had a seizure from time to time. After leaving it my life became harder and my seizures became gradually more frequent. I became less and less able to carry the burden of nervous tension and my body had much more need of relief. I ended up resorting to this whenever I was in a difficult situation.

I gave up all personal investment in high school. I couldn't follow along anymore, I felt like I was off on the moon somewhere. I needed a tutor, 24/7. Alone, I couldn't manage to study anymore. I continued going to classes, but I was just screwing around. I always had an excuse, and always a big mouth. I forced my mood and my blowups on everyone, and nevertheless I retained the sympathy of the students and the indulgence of the teachers, who liked me, even though I abused and over-abused their kindness and their patience. They tried to help me, but I was too far gone already. I was incapable of engaging my mind, of entering into any reflective process. Only the drawing classes kept me focused because I could let my brush go at will.

At the Nogent shelter, like at the high school, I had several personalities, I managed to adapt to all situations, and to all kinds of people. I got along as well with the street punks as I did with the serious students. I did some small business deals with the freaks, just trying to augment my pocket money, and we hung out in the back of the school yard to smoke dope. I felt at ease with them, there was no emotional investment in our relationships, no questions, no need to answer to anyone. With the others, the serious students, it was more complex. I wanted to be like them and integrate myself into their milieu. But when I was with them, I could sense I was an outsider, incapable of integrating, and the image of myself as a victim often jumped to mind. It was discouraging and made me lose hope of one day making it out.

There was a guy in my class whom I liked a lot. His name was Nicholas. He was a handsome, brown-haired dude with dark eyes, clean-cut. We became friends because I saved him from getting robbed. He was cool with me several times in class. Nicholas could see beyond the image I projected, he tried to find me by digging deeper. He tried helping me with my school work. He gave me lots of attention, but it was a wasted effort. It was like I was in a car whose brakes had gone and I just kept careening along. I didn't want him bothering me with his moral lessons, it hurt too much. So I kept a distance from him, to make him go away. A few years later I met Nicholas in a café at the Place de la Nation. He was handsome, mature, happy with his life. He was doing all kinds of interesting things in fashion. I stood in front of him, my life already a miserable wreck. I felt ashamed of what I was and it hurt to have him see me. I felt I came from a totally different world and, although he gave me his phone number, I made sure I lost it. . . .

When I say I had several lives, I mean my external facades and my underground lives. Inside, there was a whole flood of pent-up emotions. There was also an area about which I never wanted to think: my sexuality. Even today I have a hard time talking about it.

My experience of sex began in shame, silence, and self-degradation. I learned to make love in filth, shit, and violence. I never got to experience the soft-music-and-candles kind of mood. For me it was a power struggle, a matter of getting slapped, lied to, and betrayed. A truly wretched sex life. Just once, just one shitty time was enough. Doing it once with Jaïd was enough to make me prey for the others. In these godforsaken projects, you let yourself be taken in one single time and ever after you're screwed.

Some girls can never have sexual relations again after being raped. For others, it's the opposite. They lose all respect for themselves and start sleeping around any chance they get. That's more or less my story. What does getting laid mean again when you've suffered what I have? Does it have any significance? It means absolutely nothing anymore, just one piece of scum after another, so why stop doing it? Anyway, in my case, my body didn't belong to me after the rape. I didn't develop this attitude until after the breakup of my relationship with Mathieu. It struck me as bizarre that I could make love with Mathieu. I had the impression I shouldn't have, that it wasn't right to sleep with anyone again after a rape. But I was in love, and to make love again with a gentle, kind boy was definitely the best way to cure my wounds. However, I couldn't help but feel ashamed about it at the same time. They succeeded in shoving their stinking "principles" into the deepest part of me. Guilt, shame—I was full of it.

I was so in love with Mathieu I wanted to have a child with him. During an appendicitis operation they noticed I was pregnant. I hadn't known it myself. Obviously, I didn't want to keep it, I knew I wasn't ready. Back at the shelter, they put me on the pill. That's their policy and it's a good one. The abortion was just another ordeal under my belt. One more act of aggression on my body and my mental balance. I was all of fifteen years old. I just kept putting things under my belt without thinking about them, without trying to feel the turmoil this all caused inside me. Not only did the car's brakes let go, but on top of that the car was driving in the dark. I kept heading toward hell.

It was after my disillusionment over Mathieu's attitude that I started to "trip." That's when you go out with loads of guys at once, without necessarily sleeping with them. It was a way to avenge myself through other guys for what Mathieu did, and also to belong to no one in particular. Getting dumped is too hard! I met guy after guy on one night stands. I also had two more serious relationships that I carried on at the same time as the rest. Those were Driss and Mohammed, two main men I dated regularly for a year and a half, playing hide-and-seek between them. I toyed with everyone's feelings. I thought of myself as clever, but I always ended up in their beds.

After, I kept degrading myself without even realizing it. I only knew that what I was doing was "bad." Today, I'm ashamed and I feel badly for myself, because it's me I disrespected and debased. I got laid because I knew how to do it. I had no sense of my own worth, it didn't mean a thing. I got laid like a whore gets laid. It was a total void. I didn't realize that I was in a suicidal state and digging myself deeper into denial.

11. Algeria

Six months went by at the Nogent shelter. By then, it was the end of the school year and, in spite of everything, I passed into the next grade at the vocational high school. My mother, whom I would see away from home, offered to take me on vacation to Algeria with her and my two sisters. She wanted me to relax and clear my head. I sure needed it and I accepted on the condition that my father did not join us.

The only vacation I spent with him had been a nightmare. I still remember it. We went to La Capte on the Côte d'Azur, I must have been around twelve or thirteen. Up till then, I had always gone to my host family in Belgium. That year, however, I left with them to join my aunt and my cousins at a campground. I was happy about spending my vacation with my older girl cousins. My head was already filled with images of us having the time of our lives.

The first day, I grabbed my bathing suit and spent the whole day at the beach with them. On my return that evening, my father was absent. I took a shower and got ready to go out for ice cream. You know, the typical vacation thing! My mother had given me the green light, so there was no problem prolonging the evening a little. Then I was told that my father was looking for me and that I had to go back, which I promptly did. When I got there, he was gone. My mother told me to lie down and pretend I was sleeping. So I did it, clueless as to what I had done wrong. I had gone out for ice cream with my aunt and my cousins. What was wrong with that? After a while I heard my father get back. He was furious and picked a fight with my mother, who tried to defend me. He ignored her and headed straight for my room, shouting insults.

"*Kalba!* Where the hell are you? What were you doing out there?" He came closer and ripped off my bedcover. "Pretending to sleep, huh? That just tops it off!" This sent him over the edge: he kicked me in the face. I screamed and threw myself out of the tent, pushing past him and my mother. Blood gushed from my nose all over the place. Stunned and furious about what had just happened to me, I took shelter with my aunt, who comforted me. It was okay, my nose wasn't broken. But she defended him nonetheless, "You shouldn't have gone out without telling your father, he's right!" I couldn't get them to understand that I had been given no time to explain myself. The injustice of it revolted me. My father had kicked me in the face like you kick a soccer ball!

For someone who thought she was spending a real vacation,

80

enjoying the same freedom as my cousins, I was off to a hell of a start! If I understood correctly, he wanted me to sit next to him on the sand making patty cakes like when I was five years old. My vacation schedule was like "Wow!" Housework all morning with my mother, then turning in circles until four o'clock when my father woke up from his siesta. Finally, beach time, with him of course. To stop him from embarrassing me, I kept my cool. What a blast this vacation was turning out to be!

I was completely discouraged and, from that moment on, the more my father told me what I couldn't do, the more I acted out. He watched over my every action and gesture, he controlled every place and person I looked at. He was past the limit. I had only one desire: to make him royally pissed off, as if to tell him, "You see, your beatings have no effect! I do everything you tell me not to!" Soon, I was completely saturated by my father's constant surveillance. I couldn't take it anymore. My only thought was to get the hell out of there, to take off, escape! I wanted to show him that he didn't scare me and that I could always run off.

I disappeared for a couple of weeks. I slept in a house under construction. My cover and my mattress were two sheets of Styrofoam. For food, I shoplifted at the Monoprix in Bandol. One evening, I tried my luck at the casino bar in Bandol with the hope of getting a new picture of things and warming up a bit. The bouncer burst out laughing the minute he saw my kid's face and threw me out. He made my blood boil! Finally, my mother came and got me after two weeks on the run. She tried to smooth things out. Until next time!

That was why my only condition for this vacation back in Algeria was that my father stay home.

My mother had arranged things well. We were in Sidi Fredj, a gorgeous beach resort with a small port, historic sites, and lots of nice restaurants and bars. Perfect! We had two months of vacation reserved, one month in each of two different hotels. Awesome! Back in Algeria, though, you have to put up with their mentality. Immigrants like us are given the run around. Since the service was poor, I made some justifiable remarks, in French, which annoyed them even more. Every day, you had to negotiate to get the least thing. It was exhausting! The waiters took all kinds of liberties: one of them helped himself to my cigarettes, the cleaning woman's daughter stole my clothes and I saw her strutting around in them in town. Every day brought another headache.

It was pretty upsetting and I didn't handle it well. I was definitely in a very particular state of mind at that moment—strung out, uptight, ready to explode at the least disobliging remark. But there was only one thing that mattered to me: to remain positive, to use this vacation to forget all about K. and his cronies. I wanted to outmatch them, to beat them at this battle of suffering they had forced on me. I wanted to erase the memory of that dark year and my degrading escapades. I wanted to forget the shame of what I had become. I wanted to live, dammit! A normal life.

So, I went to the beach, out to the disco from time to time, trying to have fun like everybody else. One day at the pool, I met three boys who lived in France, not far from me. We got on well together because we had some mutual friends. Every day, they came to use the hotel pool. I was glad to have some kids my age I could joke around with.

One evening I went to smoke a joint on the beach with one of them. It was nice out, the sea was calm and sparkling, we were chatting at ease. I felt good. Suddenly, three guys appeared, presenting themselves as policemen, and without showing any IDs, they demanded to see ours. I refused to show them mine because they didn't look like cops. While we were talking, I saw one of them pull my friend aside and move far off. They disappeared.

That was when the other guys fell on me, beating me black and blue, leaving me no time to realize what was happening, hitting me with a ferocious brutality that still echoes in my head. I couldn't believe it was happening, a real nightmare. I cried out, I howled for help, I tried to flee. I ran, I fell in the sand, I got back up and ran some more, panic-stricken. They caught me and shook me up. Stunned and trembling, I was scared to death. To shut me up, they kicked sand in my mouth.

As the beating got worse, I screamed. Then one of the guys took a knife out of his jacket and showed me a big steel blade. Terrified, I shut up instantly. And then the horror started again. For the third time in my life, I became the object of their sexual cruelty, the instrument of their sadism, their cowardice, the most abject violence. While they relieved themselves on me, I talked to God as loudly as I could in my head, begging him to let me live. I begged him to spare me, because I was convinced they were going to kill me. I saw my whole life go by. I felt the approach of death. With no strength or arguments left, I bartered my jewelry for my life.

The next day, I showed up completely wrecked at the doors of the hotel. I threw a fit. My dress had been ripped to shreds, my underwear as well. I was half naked, but I didn't even realize it. My eyes, my ears, my mouth, and my hair were full of sand and dried blood. I had walked through town for a long time, dazed, lost, crying out for my mother, but it was too early, the streets were empty, everyone was asleep.

At the hotel the boy at the reception desk stared at me in incomprehension. I screamed at him to call my mother. Exhausted, I fainted, only to then wake up in my mother's arms with a lot of people standing around us. The crowd scared me and I started screaming, thinking they were my attackers. Still under shock, I lost it completely. When I had calmed down a bit, my mother brought me to the hospital to have me examined and treated. A report had to be made for the police as well. My body was riddled with bruises—on my temple, forehead, back, arms, legs, and thighs. My face was smeared in blood because of the punches I took to the mouth, my knees were split open.

I still had sand everywhere, deep down in my most intimate parts and lining my throat. I spit up sand for several days. The doctor, a woman, tried to examine me without gloves on and with the window open to the workers outside. She got a dazzling kick to her gut as I fell into a second fit. I was sick, not sick in my body because it had been anesthetized by so much beating. Rather, I was sick for my body, that poor thing, for it having to suffer so much violence. I was sick in my head from so much injustice, so much barbarity. I was sick of this overwhelming powerlessness to defend myself, to make others understand me, and especially, to believe what had taken place.

The commentaries started up again. "If anything like that ever happened to me, I'd kill myself before I gave up!" "Never in a million years would I let anyone do that to me!" and then there were my mothers' eyes which blared out what she was thinking to herself, "But it's not possible! She must go looking for it!" 'Cause I can read people's eyes like a book. There was disapproval, suspicion, sometimes a little pity, but never compassion. Everyone smeared me with the thought that it was my fault.

Later we went to the police station to file a complaint. We were received there by a bastard who couldn't give a damn about what had happened to me, about my bruises, my blood splattered clothes, my sand-filled mouth, my state of shock. He asked me intrusive questions in order to better understand, so he said, why this had happened to me. He asked, for instance, whether I was a virgin before the rapes! When I had the naïveté to answer no, he looked at me with the filthy gaze of a lecher. "Oh, well, you should have said that!" he replied. At that precise instant, I understood he wouldn't do a thing. It made me hysterical. I insisted they act. "OK, quiet down, now! You're really asking for it, little missy. You shouldn't have been out there, hanging out on the beach at that hour!" Those were the police chief's words. Still I managed to get a team to go down to the beach. With a sweater thrown over my tattered dress, I followed along. Pure humiliation.

You have to know that back home in Algeria, on the beaches, there's a daylife and there's a nightlife. A whole bunch of people, even little kids, sleep in the bushes along the sand, because they have nowhere else to go. That night, people asleep there heard my screams and didn't lift a finger. I remember passing by a man sleeping there, a bearded guy, a Muslim brother, I guess. I remember begging him to help me. He rolled over and went to sleep farther on. Tons of people, kids, came out of nowhere. All of a sudden I recognized the man with the beard and asked him to testify, figuring that, faced with the police, he'd be forced to speak up. "Me? No, I didn't see anything, I didn't hear anything, I was asleep over there in the bushes, I swear, I've never seen this girl!" A feeling of injustice and revolt rose through me and I insisted, "Please remember! I begged you to help me last night, you were sleeping right over there, I beg you, help me!" No, he didn't recognize me, didn't hear a thing. He was the guy, though, I was sure of it.

I thought of the friend who had been with me the day before on the beach; he had been found at home that morning, asleep. He said he had woken up on the beach after being knocked out a while! Need any commentaries? It was a nightmare, I couldn't believe it was happening. Would no one help me? I screamed with rage and wounded faith. The cop covered my mouth. "Alright, that's enough of that, you're starting to really annoy us!" That was when I got a kind of flash, I understood on the spot that it would come to nothing, that the whole thing stopped there. And in effect, the complaint was filed away immediately. A few days later, however, a young couple was found murdered. The boy and the girl had both been raped, their throats slashed and their guts spilled, on the same spot where I was raped. I never went back to Algeria.

I understood that there was no justice in that shithole of a country, because the police are all taking bribes. I understood immediately looking into the eyes of that cop that there was no sense in insisting, that there wasn't the least hope. I abandoned it all there when I returned to France. The two thousand kilometers that separated me from it helped me not to think about it again, to try to forget what I'd been through. I consoled myself by thinking that, at least in France, laws do count for something.

Back in France I returned to the shelter, saying nothing, of course, about what had happened to me, which nobody would have believed anyway. "Raped a third time, boy, she wants it!" That's what they'd have said, no question. Even for me, it was hard not to believe it after all these years of struggling. Was it me who suffered all that? How could I have withstood so much? Still can't get my head around that.

12. I remember . . .

It was September, I had come back from Algeria more beat-up than when I'd left. But I didn't let anything show. I didn't speak about it, I didn't cry. At the shelter, I plastered a huge smile on my face, reinforcing my armor to hide my wounds. I didn't even realize I had just spent a terrifying year of multiple traumas. In a state a shock but without realizing it, I could only watch as the gears started cranking all over again.

I soon learned that the Nogent shelter was closing down and this news upset me deeply. It had been a good place for me. Its closing pushed me even further downward, straight to hell. I found myself without a home, without a school, without work or a brain for that matter, and I wasn't even seventeen years old. What future did I have in this condition? But none of it stopped me dreaming of a job, an apartment, and a driver's license. At the time, I didn't register the impossibility of this. I was totally incapable of taking responsibility for my life.

Some of the teens in the shelter went home, others were placed elsewhere. Me, I had to wait for my social worker to find me a placement. For I now had a social worker, someone whose function, according to the juvenile court in Bobigny, was to "take care" of me. Actually, his role was limited to checking in with me from time to time and then giving me another appointment with a big "take care, see you next time!" He couldn't have cared less and just satisfied himself with lecturing me. He failed to ask himself one little question about the meaning of my behavior and never suggested I see a shrink. Not exactly someone I could count on—once again! They sure didn't come a dime a dozen, the people I could trust!

The fact that I had spent a vacation with my mother gave him ground to think that everything had returned to normal, that I could go home. He took me for a little troublemaker who wanted to run away. He'd already visited our home and was astonished not to find the usual Beur clichés: I didn't have fourteen older brothers, unemployed parents, etc. Since I didn't fit the ticket, in his eyes I had no reason to be in a shelter. When he proposed I return to my parents after the shelter closed, I refused point blank. I wanted another shelter, period. I was completely unable to confront my parents face to face, to handle the tension that constantly reminded me that I'd been raped. I'd rather have bummed around on the street than go home. It was sad!

Fact is, during that whole period, I was walking around like a zombie. I thought I was invincible, as indestructible as that material, mercury I think, that you can bend any which way and that always bounces back into shape. I thought the worst was over and that I would manage to overcome whatever difficulties I might encounter. In any event, no one seemed able to help me, and no one understood: not my parents, the social worker, or the lawyer. I longed for someone to listen to me without judging me. I wanted someone to say something that would break down the wall and let me finally unburden myself of everything I was holding back.

But how do you get someone to understand, how do you get them to believe you? What I went through there, what goes down in our neighborhoods, is crazy. My life was crazy! How could people so ignorant of the reality there understand my suffering, my shame and guilt? How could they understand the fear I felt of falling back into the clutches of my attackers and undergoing their revenge for having filed a complaint? Could they imagine the prison everyone had locked me in since the rapes, writing on me in indelible ink that I was "an easy lay, a cellar slut, a whore"?

'Cause ever since the rapes, I had had to endure the constant harassment of heartless jerks. In public places I had to put up with their insinuations, their cutting jibes, their insults. You think you can protect yourself, but all that venom digs right in, it smears you a bit more each day until you end up believing and identifying with the image they've made of you. For years, I couldn't live a normal life, I had to constantly hide. I was always on the lookout and I stayed away from places where I risked being "burned."

But one night I went to a rap concert, the first one given in France by some colossal stars. There was a great lineup. I love music and I wanted to go despite my fears. For the past two or three years I had avoided places where the music I liked was played, but that evening I was sick of hiding. So off I went. The first group up was Jungle Brothers. Everything was cool. I was so into the music I forgot what was happening around me. When the second group came out, the mood got heavy. There were problems with the sound equipment and the crowd got antsy. All of a sudden a guy came up to me. "So, how's Jaïd doing?" he said, "I got a big one too, you know. Want a lick?" I'd been grooving to the sound, moving to the music, totally laid back, when those words sent a chill right through me and froze me to the spot. There was no confusion about the situation. I noticed the guy wasn't alone, a little circle began to form around us. I could feel the panic rising in my blood. But somehow I managed to break through, disappear into the crowd, and leave the concert. I got away that time, but I felt singed.

I'm not saying that my everyday life consisted of ambushes like that, but those chance encounters, the shame of being seen as easy prey, and the fear that came with it, poisoned my days. I became a hunted animal. It lasted years, because my story spread to other neighborhoods, other burbs. Everyone knew I had had the temerity to send a "big wheel" to the joint. That's the law of the projects for you.

While I was waiting for a placement, I fell back into the same old grind. No shelter, no plan, just a profound sadness that poisoned my life. I was a total wreck. The social worker still hadn't found a shelter and I refused to go home. So I was on the street. I moved from place to place, never knowing where I'd sleep or eat. I didn't even know what I'd be doing an hour later. That's the street for you! You're the prisoner of the instant, you take whatever presents itself, good or not so good. It's hard at sixteen to find yourself homeless and alone. At the time, I didn't want to even see that it was hard; if so, I would have chickened out. If I had realized the difficulty of my situation, my emotions would have swamped me. I couldn't let that happen, I had to hold up. I went from one thing to the next without ever thinking.

At the beginning of this rough stretch, I remember squatting at Clara's place, an old friend I had met again by chance. Her parents, who were on vacation in Guyana, had left her the house. You can imagine the "village fete" that went on there every night. Tunes, booze, weed, tons of people. Nonstop partying! For Clara, it was a vacation, but for me, it was the same old dark spiral, letting myself get sucked into anything to forget the reality of my life. Shit! What I'd have given to see it all end, but it was only the vacation that ended. Her parents came home. I was back on the street.

I can also recall hanging out with some junkies for a while, guys from Villiers-le-Bel who were squatting in an apartment in Saint-Denis. It was the squat that made me go with them, not the dope. But I ended up sharing their day-to-day life: breaking into apartments, reselling whatever we could at Barbès, scouting for drugs in shabby housing projects. As for me, a little shit and a good merguez-sausage-fries-ketchup-and-mayo, which at the time cost ten francs at the Gare-du-Nord, made my day.

It's like my head is crammed with these moments, all kinds of people and experiences, one "I can remember" after another, both good and bad. "I can remember," sometime after leaving the Nogent shelter, deciding to look up my friend Salima, who had run away from the shelter with a bitch who was seriously nasty. I knew the kind of girl Salima was, all sweet and generous. Even if I had taken advantage of her for some petty thefts, I still didn't want something real bad to happen to her. Searching up and down, I learned she was hanging out near La Défense. Brazen, I headed off alone, or almost, my trusty Blade always at my side. I didn't find Salima, but I did bump into that bitch and her homeboy. I didn't back down an inch.

"You seen Salima?" The meuf was with her man, which gave her the right, so she thought, to pump it up and look down at me with her stuck-up attitude. Uh-uh! No way was I gonna let her look at me like that. Slut, I'm gonna make you eat your eyes out.

"I dunno!" Oooh! You scare me! Look, you better not fuck with me just 'cause your boyfriend's here!

"Why you want to see her anyway?"

"You the new cop around here or what?"

"Even if I knew, I wouldn't tell you!"

I thought I'd start by making her eat her teeth. She was way too pumped up. She had already tried that once at the shelter. She wanted to rule me, have me steal to keep her closet full. I sent her packing, the bitch. And there she was at it again. She was counting on her man to give me a beat down, the slut. But that wasn't how it went down. To the contrary, her guy dug it: two meufs attacking each other, what better sight! I read in his eyes that he had no desire to move, in fact he was just dying to watch the "show." To see how his homegirl, his little punkette, stacked up. Soon as I registered his look, I let loose on her, grabbing her hair and shoving her to the ground. Splayed there, I kicked her in the head and the stomach. I tried to scratch her eyes out. I kicked her ass! I wasn't going to let that bitch walk away. I managed to hold her down so I could press my knife against her cheek. I was ready to slash her face.

That's when a man passing by put a stop to it. Or rather, put a stop to me because I was about to do something really stupid. He had the courage to intervene, to yell at us and pull us apart, bug-eyed to see two girls fighting like that. And all of it under the sadistic gaze of that homeboy, who didn't lift a finger to separate us. The asshole had just stood there stone-faced.

Okay, a last "I remember," just as painful and violent. I was still on the street. My situation hadn't changed much, except that I had started hanging with a gang of girls, 'cause for a long time I had moved around on my own. Once again, I met up with them by chance. These girls and me, we were a lot alike: queens of the street, runaways, hustlers, thieves, dope fiends, boozers, punching bags for our parents, full-time brawlers, speed-daters with any bozo. We were all the same!

One night we all decided to go to the Voltage FM evening at Marcadet-Poissoniers. Dressed in shirts, jeans, and gym shoes, we were hoping not to be refused entry at the door. On the way there we stopped in a corner store to buy a little flask of whisky, which we mixed with Coke to put ourselves in the mood. The event was being held in a warehouse, and all that mattered to me was that I was plugged into some good sound. I leaned against a wall in the corner to roll a joint, after first taking a little stroll around the hall to make sure I wouldn't be having any nasty encounters. Even when I was wasted, I kept watch. The evening started without a hitch.

I don't recall how or why I got into a fight with a guy. All I remember is a punch in the face. Luckily, my nose was used to it. I answered him with a kick in the butt and my can of Coke in his face! I took advantage of his surprise to disappear into the crowd. Trying not to walk into him again, I went looking for my girlfriends, whom I found chatting up some guys from the hood, homeboys of Jaïd and K. All the bad luck in the world fell on me there. It was unreal! Our world is a village, no one's a stranger. I had to get out of there ASAP. To my total surprise, I was greeted with a "Wassup?"

It was "Creep Night." No joke. Drummed up a lot of feelings in little time. Getting punched in the mouth, meeting up with Jaïd's homeboys, not exactly the most gentle fellows. More than anything, I felt a growing, looming dread. Where was that evening of psychos leading? As creepy as it sounds, Jaïd's buddies handed me a glass of whisky, a "who cares about the past" kind of gesture. What the hell was I doing there? Clinking glasses with a bunch of bastards, one eye scanning for the shithead who wanted revenge for the butt kick and the facial humiliation I gave him. What a scene! How'd I get out of that mess? One of Jaïd's homeboys actually told the "girl slinger" to go play elsewhere. Stunning. I was still in a spin from it but very much on my guard. On my guard was all I could be, so stunned by events I couldn't think straight. And for good reason, 'cause the evening spun out of control: a general melee broke out in the hall. The music stopped, the lights went up. I saw a chair fly by, fists flung from every side, terrified people trying to flee. The brawl spilled onto the street, fed by shots fired from both sides. My girlfriends and I lay flat on the floor. We ducked the bullets whistling above our heads. Sounds like I'm describing a film, huh? Uh-uh! Fucking nuts, it was! A night for psychos. An "I gotta be nuts" kind of night.

Fights, hassles, street brawls like that one fill my head to overflowing. One chapter alone would never suffice to recount them all. But don't get me wrong, I'm not trying to brag about my exploits. I'm just testifying to the violence I lived amid. It was always the same. It would start from nothing and finish with a "Blam!" I'm not very proud of what I was at that time. Of all those brawls and screaming fits. Back then, girls like me, we weren't young women, we were little men, little soldiers, balls of fire ready to explode. Did I have a choice? I dealt with my reputation as an "easy lay" by getting into fights and spitting out the violence inside. I mistreated my body, and it suffered. I was a kamikaze, I brawled with as many girls as boys. I paid my dues. I'm no stranger to fists. I had no fear and I took as much as I gave out. My best way of intimidating people was my voice. I have a deep, loud voice that makes an impression. If it didn't suffice, I lunged!

That's what it means to have to hustle. You meet one person

after another, nice or nasty, chalking up brawls, squats, neighbor-hoods, men. You don't need long on the street to turn bad, some-times a few weeks will do. Very quickly, you lose all respect for yourself and do whatever you need to get by. You live by instinct, never stopping to think.

I kept meeting with my social worker, nonetheless, to know where he was at with finding me a shelter. No place nowhere, so far, and nothing to do but wait. From time to time, I went to see my mother at work to hit her up for some cash. It was my way of saying I existed, because I had the impression that since my departure, my parents had written me off. Then it was back to hustling—same old grind, same old mischief.

During the wait I slept wherever I could—cars, staircases, strangers' homes, godforsaken dumps. One night, I agreed to do what a guy asked in exchange for a mattress and a couple francs. When I left his place, I didn't feel good. I felt all empty and ashamed inside, like a piece of shit, a disgusting lump of filth. It was one too many times for me. Falling so low was horrifying. How I detested myself! I detested the violence that lived inside me and the sexual object I'd become, a real "cellar slut," just like they said. I saw myself as a puppet, resigned and inert, passed from hand to hand and made to do whatever anyone wanted. I was capable of following anyone I met in the street and sleeping with him. I swung from state to state: from cellar slut to brawler to smiley face to fit thrower, from nice girl to delinquent, but al-ways a hustler, a girl turning in hell! I was caught in a spiral that sucked me down. I just tried not to drown.

December 22, 1989. Three months after the Nogent shel-ter had closed its doors and I still hadn't found a place. I'd just turned seventeen, but I felt like a hundred. I was in Saint-Denis. I walked out of a hair salon retching for having spent a hundred francs for what you'd have to call a "pyramid" cut, which I tried to camouflage with my hat. I was at Place-du-8-Mai-1945. I set up house on a bench, smoking joints, watching people go by as my teeth chattered from the cold. I wanted to find someone to take off with somewhere. A guy, a girl, anyone who cared. In truth I didn't know where to sleep that night, I had to find a solution.

I was deep in thought when I saw a guy I hadn't seen for a long time. Lyes. He was driving around with his buddy Hafid. They were at the red light when our eyes met. We flashed on each other. He got out of the car to say hi, telling his friend he'd meet up with him at the gas station. I could feel he was happy to see me, and it was reciprocal. We hadn't seen each other in almost two years. The last time had been at the movies. We'd all sneaked in without paying. Definitely created some bonding. . . .

He asked me what I was doing there. I cooked up a long answer so he couldn't see I was in trouble. I told him I was waiting for a friend to show up.

"If you want, I can wait with you. That way we can keep chatting. So? Been a while since we saw each other! You hang around here?"

"Sometimes. . . . But I'm pretty much in Paris."

"And what are you up to tonight?"

"I'm not sure . . . maybe a party."

Truth is I was waiting for someone who didn't exist. How could I tell him that? So I said it different, making it better than it was. As usual, I let things drift. If he offered me something, I'd follow, if not, I'd be sure to find some hallway to crash in. And a heated hallway 'cause it was nippy outside.

"Your friend doesn't seem to be coming!"

"Can I have a swig? I'm cold."

"Aha! You like booze!"

"I like booze, shit, clubbing. Who cares? Does it bother you or something?"

"Hey, relax! I'm no fundamentalist. You do what you want, I'm no judge. Actually I like girls like that. They've got guts. They'll never let you screw 'em over!"

I liked what he'd just said. He'd been around. A girl like me, who drank and smoked, didn't shock him, 'cause he didn't know about the rest yet. Still, what he'd just said touched me, fool that I was, to the heart. Noticing that my imaginary friend wasn't showing up, he asked me to spend the evening with him and invited me to see a movie. He asked his friend to go on without him. We decided to have a drink, while we waited for a showing of *Sea of Love* with Al Pacino—everybody's godfather!—in a bar at the Place du Clichy. We shared our life stories. Course, I didn't get into the details, but I enjoyed the moment we spent together. He made me laugh. I felt good in his company, although I remained on guard. For me, nowhere was safe. At the movie theater I waited for the moment when he'd grope me under my T-shirt and take advantage of me, just like the others. I knew that tune. But nothing happened. Was he going to be different? Would he respect me? Returning on the subway, we rolled a joint, still talking. He was worried my parents would yell at me for getting back so late. I told him some crap like, "My parents are super cool!"

Giving him no clue about my life, I planted a kiss on his cheek, thanked him for a nice evening, and left him at the end of the line in Saint-Denis. Then I retraced my steps. As I walked I went over the whole evening in my head. I remembered his smile, his laugh, everything he said to me. My heart was beating like a drum. On the other hand, I tried not to have any illusions. A meuf like me is for having fun with, smoking a joint. With my file that weighed a ton, I was not the kind of meuf you stayed with, imagined a future with, or married, God forbid. I was just a meuf you shot the shit with. I was lost in my thoughts when I heard, "Where are you headed like that?" Damn! He had followed me.

"You scared me! Here we are though, almost home. It's at the end of the street."

"Oh, I see. Well, can I walk you then? That way I won't worry."

"You really don't have to. . . ."

It was the first time someone had ever worried about me. I was deeply moved. But did that mean I could trust this guy? He walked alongside me. I felt trapped. I'm screwed! How could I explain my situation to him? I didn't want to tell him I slept outside, but neither did I want to let him go. I sensed he was trustworthy. His presence felt good.

"ok, look, I lied to you! I don't have anywhere to go; I'm homeless. I don't know where to sleep. ok!"

"See! I knew something was up. That's why I followed you, to see what you were going to do. You alright? Keeping it together? Where you gonna go?"

"ok, so now you know everything. Look, I'm used to this. I'll figure it out. I'm fine! You can go home now."

"Is that what you want? I let you sleep outside somewhere, and meanwhile I go home to sleep in my warm bed, no worries! I'd be a shit to let that happen!"

"Listen, until today that didn't bother anyone. So why should it bother you?"

"I've got some dough. Let's look for a hotel, okay? But I won't touch you. I'll go home and we'll see each other tomorrow. What do you think?"

Shit! Who was this guy? Paying for a hotel room and giving me pocket money for the next day, without anything in exchange? In all these years it was the first time I'd met a guy who offered to help me without expecting anything in return. Had I finally found a shoulder to lean on?

We found a hundred-franc room in an old hotel. It was flea-bitten with roaches galore, but who cared. It'd been ages since

I'd slept, since I'd laid my head down in a safe place, so I wasn't choosy. Lyes started to leave as agreed. But I didn't feel like staying alone, so I asked him to stay. I felt like continuing the conversation. It did me good to be with someone. We tried the bed out, me playing the cool meuf, but I felt deeply uncool in fact. I watched Lyes roll a joint. He had a head like a teddy bear with an Asian slant. Big cheeks. Think whatever you want! He was no prince, but he had charm. To me, he was very attractive.

Lyes told me he belonged to a band of graffiti artists, the TWKs and the 93 NTMs, among the first groups of this kind to roam and tag all over Paris. He told me about the "events" he'd been involved in. I listened to him talk about his family, his parents, his brother and little sisters. I wished the night would never end. No more worries. Nothing but him and me.

Another joint and I unpacked it all, everything, the whole shitload of my life story. I threw in the running away, the rapes, the threats, the lawyer, the conflicts with my parents. I had a ton to say, and it soothed me to talk, to lay it out. To have someone "on my side" at my side. I had such a huge need to tell my tale. Lyes got emotional. "How is that possible? Let your own daughter sleep outside!" I believe he was the first one to find this situation intolerable and the attitude of my parents reprehensible. Watching him get indignant for me warmed my heart.

Lyes's kindness, his attentive looks, threw me for a loop. He made me want to be whole and sincere. He made me want to tell him everything about me, to give myself completely. How I wish he had been the first. How I wished I'd never met all those one-night-stand lechers. Lyes's loving eyes gradually penetrated the concrete around my heart. Though I was in serious shit, those moments with him were ones of extraordinary happiness. Even if I feared the happiness would evaporate too quickly. Lying on the bed, we kept talking deep into the night. Neither he nor I felt like sleeping. Just managing to see the outline of his face, I watched him in the dark.

"Close your eyes," he told me. "Please." I felt his warm lips press against mine. "If you don't want me to, push me away." But I had no desire to push him away. I wanted those shy, warm kisses again. I wanted his hands to keep caressing my face. I wanted to feel his breath again. I wanted this moment to never end. I wanted to offer my whole being to him. I asked him to make love. He said he didn't want to rush me. He said he hadn't helped me to take advantage of me. Wow, a guy who didn't function with his dick ready in his hand! I was taken aback, amazed. I ended up falling asleep in his arms, and sleeping, I felt his tender warm kisses on my neck. It was not a dream; it was Lyes. In the early morning, we woke up naked, enlaced in each other's arms. We had made love. It was the first time since Mathieu that I had made love with someone instead of getting laid. Lyes.

He became my partner in purgatory. During the day we did our separate things. At night he often made me dinner in secret at his place. When I didn't find a place to sleep, he stayed with me. We'd take covers and spend the night in his brother's car, a little blue Renault 5. The moments I spent with Lyes transformed the harsh edge of my troubled life. I felt good with him and that changed everything.

13. Confrontation

When I returned to my neighborhood in Pierrefitte to see my little sisters, whom my father forbid me from approaching, I learned from well-meaning people that I was not the only one who'd been "turned." Jaïd, K., and the others were reported to have participated in other gang rapes. They were thought to have a dozen to their credit. K. was supposed to have dragged a bunch of his buddies into these "exploits." I also heard stupid remarks such as:

"What, you're still alive?"

"What's that supposed to mean? 'Course I am!"

"Well, there's a rumor running around about you. They say

you were found hacked up in pieces in a dumpster! Their way of punishing you for going to the police!"

Or I heard, "You don't know? Some are saying you were looking for it, hanging around like that! And K. is going to fuck you up when he gets out of prison!" A regular "Voice of the Hood," created for the mere pleasure of badmouthing, dissing, shitting on, and especially smearing people.

I learned to distrust what people said. I knew that most of them enjoyed feeding a psychosis. There was no end to it. So-and-so said this, so-and-so said that. Those vicious rumors drove me crazy. They were like smacks in the face. At each attack, my heart beat a mile a minute. The story trailed me everywhere, leaving a large wake. I felt like one of those airplanes flying over the beaches on the Côte d'Azur in summertime, dragging an ad tied to its butt.

Some time later I was summoned to the courthouse in Pontoise, to the magistrate's chambers, for a new face-to-face confrontation with K. My mother accompanied me this time, having understood that it was a mistake to let me go alone with my father the last time. What hell it was going to Pontoise! K. was there with two lawyers just for himself, while I had only the lawyer appointed by the association, the one I couldn't stomach. My legs were like Jell-O throughout the confrontation. It was the first time I spoke in front of a magistrate, but I was not supposed to defend myself there, rather simply relate the events. We were not at the trial stage.

During the confrontation, I learned that K. had indeed been accused of several tournantes. I heard names of girls I didn't know. The Voice of the Hood turned out to be well-informed. K. lied. He ratted on Jaïd and his other friends, but said nothing about the ones who were present that night. Why? He then proceeded to paint me as a filthy slut, adding, of course, that I

had consented, almost begged him to jump me. I felt humiliated, sullied, and fouled once again. The stakes were high: it was
his word against mine. Fortunately, the magistrate defended me,
more than my lawyer, actually, who was totally out of it. . . . She
said nothing of any interest during the confrontation and didn't
even speak to me afterward. She took off immediately, shouting,
"I'm in a rush!" I never saw her again. Hard to believe? Believe it.

This confrontation was no moment of glory. I consoled myself
with the thought that everything would be different at the trial.
I fantasized asking the judge for permission to tell him what my
life had been like since that day. In the meantime I kept it all on
a front burner, waiting for the trial date. After the confrontation
my mother invited me out to a restaurant. I was not very hungry,
but I understood she wanted to make a gesture toward me and
console me. It was nice. Except that during the whole meal she
talked about the future.

"You have to put it all behind you! You have to look straight
ahead now. That's all in the past! Do you know that I believe in
you? I'm sure it's going to work out for you, believe me!" Alright,
already! The problem was I was just not there yet. What I really
needed was to let my hurt out, to speak my suffering. And she
didn't give me a chance. "Eat! Eat! Stop worrying, you have to
stop thinking about it, you're making it worse. Think about tomorrow!" So I fell silent, and I ate. Did I have a choice?

In any case none of this had much importance. There was only
one thing that mattered: the trial. I expected a lot from that trial.
First of all, that justice would be handed down. And that K. and
his gang would be punished. I wanted to retrieve my lost dignity.

While waiting for the trial, I roamed around, same old grind.
Between two periods on the street, I stayed at some shelters.
Gambetta, where I didn't stay long. It was a shelter for addicts
with bars on the windows. Créteil, another dismal place where

you're one of a million. Aubervilliers, Pelleport, Montreuil, Crimée . . . I wanted another shelter like Nogent, with a cool attitude toward rules, but apparently they weren't easy to find. I met social workers. I told my story over and over, zapping around a bit. There were too many memories that came up each time I interviewed at a shelter. I'd had enough of talking about the rapes. Sometimes I knew the shock would be too much for them. Often I didn't fit, I didn't fall into the house criteria. Was it my story they didn't like? When I did suit them, they and their retarded rules didn't suit me.

Finally! My social worker found me a spot in a shelter in Charenton. A home for girls, though, girls only! Made me uncomfortable, but I had no choice. I was starting to get tired of the nomad life. My epileptic fits were increasing. I exploded at the slightest thing. A wrong word and it was a head butt. I didn't talk, I hit. I hit because I didn't have any words. They were smothered in my throat by the suffering I felt. I hit because I didn't see anything anymore. I was blinded by pain.

In order to stay in Charenton and benefit from a housing grant, I had to have a plan. What does it mean to "have a plan"? I couldn't make them see that I was exhausted and couldn't go another inch. I wanted to rest and empty my brain. But I couldn't find the words to say it. Their language was no different from what I'd heard everywhere else. Same old tune: sit tight, think of the future, have a plan. Parents, magistrates, social workers, lawyers! Motherfuckers! I didn't want to hear any more of their repetitive, moralizing hogwash.

I played for time. I said I was making progress. In truth I spent my days drinking and smoking with Lyes. I was in no state to look for work. I didn't have the heart for it. My only desire was to get high. In order to forget. . . . At the shelter, there was just one girl I dug, Nina. She was a gorgeous Chilean with long jet-black hair, dark almond-shaped eyes that sparkled with mischief, and a little beauty mark on the corner of her mouth that accentuated her lips. She was a real beauty and a regular home wrecker. The same thing had happened to her that had happened to me: she was gang-raped. She paid a high price for her beauty, just like me. I'm not saying that I'm a bombshell, but the little I had was destroyed by them. Nina was the only one who dared to get close to me. At night she'd come smoke a cigarette with me. She confided in me, and I told her about the happiness I'd found meeting Lyes.

They quickly deduced that I was not making any effort to find a school or a job and since it was clear I was becoming a real threat for the other girls, they soon showed me the door. So I left the shelter and Lyes invited me to live with him in a housing project in Saint-Denis. His mother, very concerned about my situation, agreed that I could live with them. She was a courageous, generous woman. I respected her a lot. She shared everything with her children and me. Lyes had a big brother, Razhee, and two younger sisters, Insaf and Jouda. Insaf was my age, just a month older, while Jouda was a little younger. Lyes's parents were separated. His dad lived in Tunisia but he returned to France now and then to spend time with his kids. I rediscovered the warmth of family life with them and it did me good. Those people opened their door to me, fed me, showed me attention and love. They welcomed me like their own daughter. And on top of that they adopted me without posing the least question. I was bowled over by so much caring. Did I deserve so much generosity and love?

My stay with Lyes was marked by several epileptic fits. Terrifying seizures. I had up to eight a day. I spent my time doing round-trips to the hospital, but I couldn't stay there. My fits expressed what no one wanted to know. My hatred exploded, my fury at the injustice to which I'd been subjected, the humiliation I'd endured. I gave it all full vent with my screams. My body, turned rock hard, trembled so much it lifted off the ground. I drooled like a wild animal, I injured myself, slapping and scratching my face. Lyes and his family were dumbfounded, terrified by what they saw. At night I also had nightmares. My howls woke up the whole house. In the morning Jouda would mention my dreams with great delicacy and tact.

Today, I believe this dangerous, destructive attitude was the only way I had to get attention and pity. It gave me the impression I was loved. It was the only means I had, like a grenade in my mouth, a way to vomit up this suffering that suffocated and devoured me so physically it was as if I were being eaten up by worms.

There was just one problem with Lyes's family. His father didn't like his girls to "hang out," and that held for me too. I wasn't used to obeying anyone anymore, I came and went as I pleased. So I had to make up some story every time I went out, or when I wanted to smoke a cigarette or a joint. Lyes and Insaf covered for me. One day, when I was down outside the apartment block chatting with Lyes and his friends, his father returned in his car. He saw me smoking and talking with the boys. We weren't doing anything bad, but he was very upset because I had failed to show him respect. He told Lyes I had to leave their home. Which I did immediately. I didn't blame the man at all. I understood his viewpoint and I was grateful to him for doing much more for me than most people. Lyes then helped me find another place. I stayed with a girlfriend of his, and we splurged on a hotel room when we had some cash. From time to time I'd stop off at my parents, but never to stay there.

14. That Damn Bag!

My mother informed me that she was leaving for Algeria with my sisters. Since my father was on vacation in Morocco, she could leave me the house all to myself. I was under no illusions, if my mother was leaving me the house keys for the summer, she had an ulterior motive. She wanted to win me back, and that meant returning to the fold. She also felt ashamed that I had chosen to live with Lyes's parents, total strangers. What must they think of her! She succeeded in getting chummy with Lyes's mother by getting to know her and showing her she was a good mother. I was used to that little game. She always tried to prove that I was at fault, not her. Her refrain went, "You're a difficult kid, hard-headed and moody." She always projected this image of me and it caused me a lot of grief. It wasn't me. Lyes's mother remained suspicious, realizing that something wasn't quite right about my mother's attitude.

In any case I was tired of the street, the dope, the alcohol, of crashing here and there, of my exhausting epileptic seizures. I needed to get my feet on the ground, and I had no alternative but to return home. I told myself that maybe things had changed at home, that events had made them think differently about things, and that maybe I'd be given more understanding.

So I returned home a few days before everyone left for vacation. No one paid attention to what I did, except for maybe my sisters. I came and went, but I didn't feel like hanging outside anymore. I spent the whole day smoking joints and watching TV. I only went out when Lyes called me. I spent a lot of time alone with my self-destructive thoughts. My parents didn't realize the gravity of my depression. There was nothing human in me anymore, no laughter, no tears, no gentleness, and they never even noticed it. They stopped at what they saw: a wild animal that howled its suffering, that threw insults and screamed in protest, that twisted in pain during sensational epileptic fits.

My mother thought I had a nervous disorder just like her brother. Right, and that's why she had a regular pharmacy of her own in her bureau drawer! My father ignored me. He floated around the place with a "nothing ever happened" attitude. I hovered like a ghost, invisible to everyone. They let me disintegrate like a piece of garbage. I felt myself sink, sliding softly toward a form of insanity that pulled me ever closer. I was torn between wanting to go toward it and wanting to die. I was hurting too much. I didn't know what hurt me more: the rapes, my life, my parents, or the troubles I was starting to have with Lyes. I was clueless. I just felt a mound of worms slowly devouring me, my head vibrating to the point of bursting with blinding pain.

One afternoon when I was home alone, I took my mother's sleeping pills from her drawer. I threw them in my mouth, one by one, like Tic-Tacs. Not seeing any effect, I took a whole handful, then another two. Finally, I fell unconscious. I slept for two days. No one at home noticed anything, nobody put two and two together. I was awoken by the telephone. I heard it echo in my head and had the impression it had been ringing for ten days. I had to answer it, but I couldn't manage to get up. My eyes stayed shut, like they were glued tight. I tried to get up and drag myself to the phone. Impossible. My legs couldn't hold me up and I fell on my face. I had to get to the phone. With superhuman effort, I succeeded in grabbing the handset. It was Monique, Fabrice's girlfriend, a friend of Lyes. "Hello, what are you doing today?" My head was in such a spin, I couldn't open my mouth to speak. I had a huge urge to vomit.

"It's bad, Monique . . . I took some pills!"

"What for?"

"To die, Monique."

"No one's with you there?"

"Naaaw!"

I was so groggy I couldn't even speak. "Don't move, I'm coming over and I'm sending an ambulance!" A little later, I was in "full form" at the Delafontaine Hospital. In full seizure, that is. I insulted and hit the nurse who wanted to hospitalize me. "I hate hospitals! I don't want to stay here! Get your dirty hands off me!" The doctor spoke to me about suicide attempts and the need for a stay in a psychiatric ward—this calmed me immediately. I was scared, very scared. There was no way I was going into that world. Despite everything that had happened to me, deep down inside, I had a desperate will to live. I was convinced something good awaited me. I just couldn't find the door that led there.

I wanted to send a message to my parents by swallowing those pills, but I screwed it up. They saw me sleeping for two days and never started to worry. They signed for my admittance into a psychiatric clinic, an annex of Ville-Évrard. I didn't belong there. The people were depressed like me, but most were truly ill, total wrecks. It was like a nonstop trauma: some people were in unbearable states, and the way they were treated was even more unbearable. We were all mixed up together, unwilling witnesses and spectators of each other's fits of insanity. How could one get better in such a place? Once again, I felt I was being punished and misunderstood.

"I shouldn't be here! I know what my problem is!"

"I'm listening to you, miss."

I told my story, worked up over having to tell it again and not be understood.

"That's why I'm suffering."

The treatment: little morning pills and little night pills.

The doctor could not allow my suffering to explode, so he found an answer: he put me to sleep. No one had heard of psychotherapy around there. He was another one to fail to understand me. I was like a poor victim dragging around a duffle bag of emotions, filled to bursting, which I kept stuffing as my destiny unfolded. That damn bag! I asked for my drawing materials. That helped me hold on, because I had no visitors. No one had time for me, not even Lyes. Once again I was alone facing a new situation, all alone with my damn bag. I swallowed this ordeal like I'd swallowed the rest. I drowned the pain, but I defended myself with all my strength against the judgments, the looks, the labels I was stuck with: "crazy," "bad nerves." It wasn't my nerves that were shattered, you bunch of bastards, it was my heart! It was hemorrhaging from lack of love, from your incapacity to grasp my pain! I defended myself with my seventeen-year-old soul. Deep down, there was a light, a tiny spark of light that resisted. It would find a way out of this tunnel one day, shining twice as bright. Despite all the crap thrown in my face, I held on to this hope.

Upon leaving the hospital I went home to my parents. Finally, my father talked to me! He wanted to know if I was eating. It was easier for him to approach a mentally ill girl than a rape victim. As far as my mother was concerned, I was sick. Not the flu or the chicken pox, mind you! I was sick in the head. Still, she pushed me to "forget everything," to "look ahead." Ahead of what? I just kept filling my bag with the whole hodgepodge of baffling behavior, destructive disappointments, isolating silences, and the stupidity I could not fathom.

15. Hell-bent

Finally, they left on vacation! They'd forget all about it. I would do the same: I forgot, denied, numbed out all the upheaval with the help of joints. Dope was my best friend and I consumed it to excess. It was in charge of me, it thought for me. It was my partner in pathos who drew me to its bed of fumes and drowned me in dark thoughts, destroying me with each lick of its flame.

Summertime, two months of vacation. It was the first time I had stayed at home. That year, I had the whole place to myself. Awesome! I could already see me and Lyes enjoying an evening with friends, him cooking up some food, then roaming around, going to the beach, doing lots of fun stuff together. In reality nothing of that sort happened. I spent my days waiting for him to return. A day with him was simple. He got up and got dressed. When he was ready, and when I'd ranted enough because it was vacation and we were doing nothing and I really had to get out, he would leave supposedly for an hour to deal with some stuff. Evenings, he'd still not be home, and I'd have spent my day champing at the bit, ready to explode in his face when he returned. As soon as I saw him, I'd badger him a little, but I quickly dropped it because he promised me everything I wanted. To keep me quiet, he'd found the best solution was dope. He was my regular supplier, which meant I now waited all day for him, all alone, and left him in peace. Even more so because he promised me we were leaving soon for vacation on the coast of Spain!

Since I was tired of waiting for Lyes and being alone, I ventured out into the neighboring park. There I met up with old friends who'd taken up dope like me. So I hung out with them smoking. Some who knew about my story wanted me to tell it, others made light of it. They were just happy to see me again. I'd changed. No one was going to screw me over again, those who tried got a swat in the face. It was over with. Never again would I let anyone power trip on giving me a lesson in this city. I'd suffered too much here!

Once I got into a fight with a guy. I hammered him and then told him I was going to get my boyfriend. When I came back with Lyes, he burst out laughing. "But Sami," said Lyes, "it's over, you beat him up, you've broken his nose, what more can I do!"

I was blinded by the need to recover my dignity. I took advantage of the time I spent hanging out in the park to put things back in perspective and do a little personal publicity. I wanted to refute all the false rumors running around about me and spread the truth. I needed to tell everyone I was the victim, not my attackers. In reality people couldn't have cared less about my emotional fits or my suffering. They just wanted to know what was what.

There was a guy who came to the park a lot named Dimitri. He was new to the hood and wasn't aware of my rep. He came from Toulouse where he'd been living with his aunt. He was studying for a diploma in enology, the science of wine. Toulouse has nothing in common with the burbs around Paris where I come from. Dimitri now lived with his mother in the same neighborhood as K. and Jaïd and the others. Despite the mood over there, he succeeded in making up his own mind about me without being misled by the others. Dimitri was a decent guy, calm, discrete, someone you could talk with. We'd meet up at the park and spend entire days smoking and shooting the shit. Soon we were inseparable. One day, I opened up about my story because I knew it was dangerous for him to hang with me. The guys in his hood who knew K. could use it to avenge themselves, and I didn't want him to get into any crap because of me.

"So there you have it, the whole saga!"

"I hear you, Sami, but you know, what happened before I got here, it's none of my business. There are people who've asked me why I haven't screwed you yet. They think that if you hang with me, it's 'cause you're looking for something. I told them I have nothing to do with this whole story and that you got nothing to worry about with me."

"They did? People told you to screw me?"

"Sure! We've been hanging out awhile, tons of people see us together. But I don't care about that. All I see is that you're decent with me, you act normal."

"Why didn't you say anything?"

"What would be the point? It's all just a bunch of hot air, but it's nice you got worried for me, I appreciate you being up-front."

Our friendship was sealed that day. There was never any ambiguity about our relationship. He never judged me or condemned me. He was my friend.

After the fight in the park with the guy I beat up, I didn't feel like returning. I could have gone around bragging about it, 'cause I sure beat the shit out of that prick! I could have savored his humiliation. Given a lesson by a meuf, and especially when the meuf in question is me, what could be worse? But no, I preferred to stay home with Dimitri. We smoked, talked, made snacks, listened to tunes, laughed ourselves silly. It was summertime! Dimitri was impressed by the amount of dope I consumed, smoking as I did from morning till night. I preferred dope to the medications they gave me at the hospital. I didn't want to look like a zombie. Take your goddamn horse drugs for the mentally ill and leave me in peace, I have my own remedy! Pot let me fall asleep and smother my pain. It grew larger day by day and I buried it joint by joint.

Luckily Dimitri was there. . . . Alone, I'd have lost it completely. Lyes didn't care much about me anymore. The time when we had shared everything was long gone. He lived his life with his friends and me with Dimitri. He got home later and later. I didn't know how he spent his days or nights. Something had changed between us, but he never let on, never told me anything, didn't want to share. He acted nice when he wanted a squeeze, but that was it. I didn't realize it was the sole reason he stayed with me and I hung onto the semblance of tenderness it represented. I gripped it like a buoy, a rotten piece of wood floating on the sea, the sea of my despair, the sea of my life.

When he had to leave, I threw hysterical fits, screaming like a madwoman. He calmed me down by saying he was making money to pay for our trip to Spain. Lyes wanted me to stay at home while he got his kicks. It seemed he even wanted me to be happy about it. He played me, manipulating me even more easily than normal because I was half-baked, lacking any discernment whatsoever. But I hadn't taken all those punches to the head in order to let someone, even Lyes, lock me in my own home. Without it ever being said, a compromise was reached: he lived his life, and I lived mine. We just met up for sex.

It was the end of summer. Everybody came back all happy, having spent good vacations. I stayed at home and my father returned to his usual behavior. Once again, he was there with his exasperated looks and his insults. It was true I had no consideration for him whatsoever. I lived my life, I came and I went. I was back to my hell-bent routine. Nina, my friend from the shelter in Charenton, hadn't forgotten me. She proposed I share an eleven-square-meter apartment with her in Saint-Mandé. She was good for me, made me laugh, full of spunk. She gave me a makeover and took charge of my fashion statement. I felt a little prettier.

Lyes came to see me from time to time for a little cuddle, but I was suspicious of him and kept my distance. One day, he courageously announced by phone that he was leaving for Spain with his buddy Yacine and that I was not invited. It was a mean blow. I felt I'd been stabbed in the gut. Spain was our little thing. I had always dreamed of romantic getaways with Lyes. My disappointment was huge, but I didn't let on. I buried the pain like a deep secret. I stayed with him, but something was broken between us for good.

After this new disillusionment, I decided to get my own kicks. With Nina, I went barhopping wherever the cover was waved for girls. It was a party every night. We went from club to club, encountering the creepiest characters in those notorious Parisian nightclubs, the most superficial weirdos you can imagine, all more or less perverse, people searching for God knows what. My thing was dancing, I loved to dance. I got down with hip-hop dancers, copying their moves and combining them in new ways. I ranked! What a show off!

And then, with Nina, it was a pigeon hunt for who would buy us a drink, a cigarette, or the cover to a club. Sometimes, we snatched a guy's wallet, other times I learned to hustle, to grind a little for dough. It wasn't my thing to make small talk, since I could tell they only wanted my ass and it disgusted me. That's when Nina would usually take the lead and I'd follow up behind.

I didn't tell Lyes about my escapades, he lived his life, I lived mine, period. I still hadn't digested the "I'm going to Spain with my buddy" thing and I swore to avenge myself by profiting from all opportunities that presented themselves. One night, the perfect one did: his name was Mourad, a guy from Montparnasse who was doing his military service. That weekend, he was on leave. We were at La Scala, one of the worst dives in Paris. The DJ played the same loop twenty times over. I was dying of boredom. But it was better than being holed up in Saint-Mandé. I let Mourad flirt with me. He played the bad boy, but no one was fooled. Mourad was no caillera, it was written in his genes, his way of speaking and holding himself. I saw him again several times when he was on leave. One night, a girl from Lyes's housing project saw us together and wasted no time spreading the news. For several weeks Lyes gave me hell to know the truth about our relationship.

"People saw you in a bar with some dude, and you tell me it wasn't you!"

"It wasn't!"

"Look me in the eyes and tell me it wasn't you!"

"It wasn't me!"

I told a boldfaced lie, I laid it on as thick as possible, pure bullshit. I wanted to bail myself out. I warned Mourad that my guy was nervous and that he must deny it point-blank if he grilled him. Lyes forced me to call Mourad. He wanted to know if he was really just a friend. That evening, there was a packed concert at Saint-Denis. When Mourad arrived, Lyes joined us and drew him away for a chat. I didn't hear what they were saying, but I watched it. Lyes gestured wildly, Mourad didn't flinch. It must have driven Lyes nuts that Mourad didn't flinch. He must have been telling himself, "How could she go out with such a fag?"

A friend of Lyes, then two, then four, approached to add their two cents. It was now a frigging tribe assembled to debate and editorialize.

"Come off it! You're not going to hit him for a ho! Check it out! He's already shitting in his pants!"

Lyes, who wanted to resolve the business discretely, got freaked that his friends were all there. So to save face, he threw a whopping punch at Mourad. It was a real zinger, deeply humiliating for Mourad who still didn't flinch. "Get the fuck outta here!" And there went my perfect opportunity, his cheek enflamed and his eyes burning with rage.

A few days later, Lyes came to see me and we made up despite the doubt that continued to gnaw on him. Life continued, in parallel. Each time Lyes grilled me, I denied everything and we stayed together. I returned to my habits, tripping, flirting with guys left and right. I thought one of them might help me forget my disappointment with Lyes and give me more love and attention. But I sure wouldn't find what I was looking for in a bar. I let myself get roped in, passing from one thing to another, never asking any questions. I just thought about getting my kicks and zoning out.

Once I disappeared for several days without telling anyone, even Nina didn't know where I was. Lyes looked everywhere, the clubs, the hospitals, the police stations. No result. When he'd been looking for me for two or three days, he found a photo of me in a magazine with a glass of champagne in my hand. I was riding high in some Parisian club. "But, that's Sami! That bitch! Two days I've been looking for her and here she is getting wasted! That meuf is driving me nuts!" When I got back, he grilled me:

"Where were you? Who were you with? Why? How come?"

"I was with some friends I've known a long time, they're squatting in a guy's apartment in the 16th Arrondissement. That's all, I swear!"

I felt guilty for the lies I had made him swallow because he took the trouble to look for me.

"Now wait a minute! Here I've been looking for you everywhere and I accidentally see your face in a magazine! Getting wasted! How twisted is that? When I think of you always complaining how bored you are here, this sure doesn't look like it!"

I felt like screaming at him, "You're the one who started this!" But I said nothing. The words rattled around my head, but the cries of protest never left my mouth. To the contrary, I served him up another batch of whopping lies, a whole truckload of ad-libs. I stood my ground: I said nothing about what I did or the people I was with. "Since you don't want to share anything with me, I won't tell you anything, and I'll go out to bars, to movies, with anyone I want. Why should you enjoy yourself behind my back and not me?" Eye for an eye, sin for a sin! Such was the end result of our relationship.

From that moment on, it made no sense at all. I hadn't forgiven him for abandoning me at the hospital and all summer long, when I needed him the most. I didn't say anything, I just swallowed it. I wasn't happy, but I was still hanging on to that dead wood. Yet nothing I got from Lyes consoled me, warmed my spirit, allowed me to grow up or embellish my life. All I got was indifference and a neglect so total it made me react like a slut. Suspicion had taken root between us. We led a kind of mental battle whose weapons were nastiness, lies, and verbal brutality.

My whole life was hell-bent, lacking any structure or foundation. I got drunk on dancing, alcohol, one-night stands, trying to fill the void of love. My head was swirling. I had no idea what day it was, what month, even what year. I forgot my age, I lived by instinct. These months barhopping exhausted me. Quarrels with Nina got worse, the hassle finding food too, and we hadn't paid the rent in ages. Our friendship wore down, I was oversensitive and she couldn't take my brutality and my impulsiveness anymore. She grew distant and it made me sad, but what could I do?

I was sick of the stupid games I played at night. In clubs, I felt like I was throwing myself to the lions, or onto an electrified fence. Guys looked at me. "Are you good for it or what?" All this bullshit to get in bed with you! But I played the game, giving in to this masquerade despite the disgust I felt for it. I didn't feel I belonged, once again. I felt smothered, asphyxiated, trapped in a world I hated, with no exit. I felt like a wounded bird desperately searching for a place to land.

16. Saint-Denis

I persuaded myself to return to my parents for good. Whatever they said, I'd stay. My father festered in his corner, watching me move in again. He threw me hate-filled looks and swore at me, "Piece of shit!" Or he snorted as loud as a bull, the sign of a huge annoyance that terrified me. In any case he never spoke to me. He'd lost his allies and found himself isolated now. The situation had changed. My sisters had grown up and my mother had gone through a physical and moral transformation. Since working in a boutique in Saint-Germain-des-Prés, she'd become a liberated woman. Her co-workers helped her come into her own. She dressed with a lot more class and didn't have the same attitude toward life. And this had changed the mood at home. She had succeeded in protecting my sisters from my father's brutality. "You won't do to the last two what you did to Samira!"

On that side of things, my father had calmed down and, as a result, my sisters had a better image of him. They approached him much more easily, especially the youngest. She was his jewel. With her, he was attentive, affectionate, devoted. Was it possible that this man was the same one who despised, insulted, neglected, and beat me? I must have really been the bad seed. From the height of her tiny frame, my little sister was the only one who could make my father stop. When she felt his spite about to lash out at me, she glued herself to my side and wouldn't let go. I heard my father's exasperated breath when he saw he couldn't attack me anymore. At home my little sister was my best protection.

My parents moved. They were forced to sell the apartment in Pierrefitte. The pressure of the gang's threats became unbearable for us all. They now lived in Saint-Denis, and me with them, of course. I was closer to Lyes, but what did that change? Between us the situation was still the same. I quarreled with him because we didn't do anything together and I continued to drug myself with his promises. But now, all respect between us had vanished.

"Where you going? Gonna go sell your ass?"

"Fuck off!"

An example of our daily exchanges . . .

Not living in Pierrefitte anymore did not cure me, of course, but the environment was different and that did me good. I was less scared to go out, less fearful of reprisals. I tried to remake my life here. I hung out in a neighborhood near the train station where I had relatives. I spent my days in a housing project with one of my cousins and his friends. I preferred to stay there doing nothing, getting high and kidding around, than being squished between a father with a constant frown and a mother who acted like nothing was up. I could "hang" in this neighborhood only because I had my cousin to protect me. 'Cause here as elsewhere, a meuf had no reason to hang out in the street. Thanks to my cousin, I could establish my "street attitude" in the new hood!

One night I counted my lucky stars for his protection. We were on our way to a bar at La Défense. We were all having fun in the RER when, suddenly, I felt someone eyeballing me. I turned my head: it was a friend of K. Getting into the train, I had done my little inspection as usual, my eyes transformed into radar with 360-degree rotation. I knew this one by sight. Built like a tank just like K. He didn't stop starring at me, even to blink. I was getting scared and discretely warned my cousin. "Don't worry about him," he assured me, "You're with us, he won't touch you!"

We arrived at the Gare-du-Nord and all got up to get off the train. When I passed by him, he suddenly pulled my arm and quietly ordered me to stay with him. I was amazed by his brazenness and froze on the spot. My cousin looked around for me and turning, saw us. I was completely nailed to the spot and the guy was gripping my arm.

"What are you doing? She's with us!"

"I know her, don't worry, cousin."

"Yeah, well, I know her too."

"Don't worry, cousin, she's staying with me, we're going to spend the evening together."

I was speechless. He grabbed me tighter and tighter as my cousin pulled my other arm, each of them pulling me in different directions like a rag doll.

"I don't think you get it, she's not going anywhere."

It was Momo, my cousin's friend, who spoke up. He was adorable, though sometimes a little cuckoo. They almost came to fists. The creep understood quick that he wouldn't be a match.

He gave up, but still didn't admit he was beaten. "Till next time!" his evil eyes told me. I felt embarrassed to have caused all the fuss. They must have taken me for a quarrelsome meuf. When would I stop trailing this past? As usual, I played the clown, the little street punk, trying to mask my discomfort and the huge fear I felt.

I thought I was protected by my cousin, but I had almost gotten caught again that time. I realized they could catch me anywhere at any time. Who could fight against a mentality? It was just wind in your head! You couldn't punch it in the face! No one could protect me from it and it didn't let up. I was damned to live with daily stress, constantly on guard. Fear had become my way of breathing. Each time I tried to live a little, there was always some jerk reminding me where I came from.

I stuffed this story in my bag of traumas along with the other hard-knock stories and all my feelings of fear, hatred, guilt, shame, and powerlessness. It all squirmed and wrapped together like a bunch of snakes and formed a chain of knots. But in other respects, I still felt good in the new neighborhood. People there understood that I hung out just to smoke and joke around with them. We enjoyed dissing each other, a national sport in the projects. It was a delicate game that required brain and imagination. A real showdown! I sometimes cried laughing or just cried, when the dissing got to be too much. Some people had a hard tongue and a killer dis. That was my main diversion. I laughed till my joints ached. I forgot everything and got back late to avoid meeting my parents. Every morning, when I woke up, I heard, "ok, get up! You're not going to sleep all day long. C'mon, move it! You came back, so now it's up to you to find a job or some kind of job training. Do something! You're not going to spend the whole day on your butt!"

"Get out, leave me alone!"

That was the short version! Every morning, I merited the un-cut, super long version!

My mother couldn't understand that I didn't want anything from her, that I took everything she said to me as an aggression. I couldn't even stand the sound of her voice in my head. When she tore into me, it was like she tore off all the pretty wallpa-per hiding the cracks. Thinking she was helping me, she tore me apart. "Act like nothing happened! You have to move on!" I sim-ply needed her to recognize my suffering.

I didn't want to talk to my parents. It was too late. Talking to them would have meant forgiving them. I did the minimum for a roof and a mattress. I disguised my sorrow by acting aggressive. My whole being was papier-mâché. I was contradiction personified.

17. My "Trial" . . .

February 21, 1991.

"Sami! Telephone for you!"

"Who is it?"

My mother lowered her eyes and handed me the receiver without a word. Strange . . .

"Hello?"

"Hello, Samira! I'm the magistrate who submitted your case to the Pontoise courthouse. Do you remember?"

"Yes, I remember you."

"I'm calling because the trial took place, and I'm curious to know why you chose not to appear."

"..."

My breath was taken away, and I couldn't get a word out. I immediately grasped the consequences of what had happened. For me, no justice. My mouth would be sealed for good. My last hope had just evaporated. A sharp heat poured through me. My head rang and a huge desire to smash everything I could see came over me. Unfortunately, I knew that wouldn't solve anything. I was totally lost. Like I was standing in front of a firing squad, already agonizing from knife wounds inflicted all over my body, and someone had just fired a bullet into my heart to finish me off for good.

"But no one told me the trial was taking place!"

"You didn't receive the summons?"

"No."

"Your lawyer didn't inform you?"

"No. My mother tried to reach her several times and she always said, 'It's following its course.' Can I appeal? Explain that no one told me the trial was taking place?"

"No, only the defendant can do that."

I was livid. This was too much! If I understood correctly, I had no other choice than to swallow it and close my mouth!

"How much did they get?"

"You know, dear, I'm not supposed to do what I'm doing. . . . I was surprised to not see you at the hearing. A colleague of mine was the presiding judge. I was surprised because you had seemed so resolute about testifying."

"I was, I still am! Sir, could you tell me how much they got?"

He obviously understood the impact of the error committed and told me what I wanted to know. He was a decent guy, for a magistrate. "The trial took place on February 21, 1991, at the Juvenile Criminal Court in Pontoise. K. was sentenced to eight years in prison, and the M. brothers to three years with eighteen months suspended sentence. I'm sure that if you had been there, they would have received more. There's no question! I don't understand what could have happened." Me neither. But what struck me as completely unbelievable was my lawyer's behavior. Not informing me of the trial date appeared like a monstrous professional and human blunder.

"Did Clarisse and Pauline appear?"

"Yes, they were there. Actually, there were about a dozen others, I believe. Do you know Claire, Latifa, Laetitia, Lara, Julie . . . ?"

He listed a dozen girls by their first names. K. took only eight years for so many first names! What was the sense in protesting? The dice were thrown.

"No, I don't know them."

"What are you up to now," he asked, trying to divert the conversation. "Still studying?"

"No, I'm not doing anything."

"You still live in Pierrefitte?"

"No, Saint-Denis now. Is that normal that she didn't call me, the lawyer?"

"Listen, dear, call her and see what happened, okay? I have to go now, take care! And . . . good luck!"

"Thank you, Mr. Magistrate."

Quick! A joint! A reefer so fat it can break the shock wave plowing through me! Quick, quick, I have to bury everything! Should I think about what just happened? Never. Control myself, yes, control myself, that was the sole thing to do. Stifle my screams, my tears. Push back this ball that wanted to shoot out of my mouth like a cannon. Bury this gigantic impotence, this hate. Numb myself to destroy the rage that was drowning me.

I was a ruin before that phone call. After, I was an apocalyptic desert. A place where my soul wandered alone, the soul I cradled in white smoke. Once again, my old friend marijuana drew me down onto its bed of fumes, and there I lay, lost in the immensity of my desert and my inconsolable grief.

Two days went by before my mother finally received the summons for the trial from the Saint-Denis police. . . . Because we had moved, the Pierrefitte police had had to undertake a search to locate us. Very well, a postal delay, that can happen! But how was it that my lawyer, who was supposed to defend rape victims, had not contacted me either before or after the trial?

I wanted to call her, but I didn't trust myself. I was afraid of losing control, of screaming and insulting her, the bitch! I felt so much hatred I was sure to act like a wild animal. I wouldn't have been able to contain myself enough to not say something that killed her, that stabbed her heart like she had stabbed mine. Instead, I preferred to drop the whole affair. I was too wasted to undertake anything meaningful. Fighting against the justice system . . . I knew that tune, "Justice, the system stinks. . . ." Fight for what? For whom? For me? Since what I'd heard a few minutes ago, I had ceased to exist. I'd lost the courage to move all those mountains: the lawyer, the judge, the associations, etc.

I was through listening to people talk. I wanted to sink into my troubles, get high, and forget. I could have shot myself, but that would have meant they had won. And I didn't want that at any price. I despaired that there was no justice anywhere, neither here nor in Algeria.

Neither the lawyer nor the association returned my mother's calls. My mother took it upon herself to play the detective. She gathered from various sources that it was not the lawyer who appeared on the day of the trial but a young intern from her office. Ms. Lawyer was at the winter sports stadium! The intern knew nothing about the case, because he'd been given an empty folder the day of the trial. He was flabbergasted: a gang rape being tried at the criminal court, not an everyday affair! I also learned that during his closing speech, the prosecutor asked for a sentence of twelve years for K. because he was the instigator. He only got eight, which is much too little when you subtract the time held in custody and remission. The M. brothers had done time in custody and benefited from a suspended sentence because they had jobs. Jaïd was also sentenced to six years in prison for gang rapes with others, including K. I cannot begin to understand why rapists and pedophiles get less than bank robbers. Is it less serious to rob people than banks?

Do you know that after this business, I the victim was sentenced to fourteen years in my head, fourteen years trying to understand and overcome it, fourteen years reconstructing myself? I battled fourteen years straight.

The lawyer didn't even send me a summary of the verdict, so I had to ask for one at the courthouse. I received a cold piece of paper, the only trace of "my" trial. It added the final touch to killing me. I froze reading this line: "K. is sentenced to pay a symbolic franc in damages and interest to the Such-and-Such Association. . . ." My life wasn't worth more than a franc? I was denied a trial and my only consolation was this symbolic franc that the association demanded of these scumbags. For, in fact, the lawyer represented the association, not the victim, who got nothing. She defended the association's interests, not mine. The intern spoke in the name of the association, not in my name. And besides that, my name did not even appear anywhere in the ruling. Only the names of the association, the intern, and the attackers were cited. I simply did not exist.

What I knew about my trial was a series of bits of information, gathered here and there from indirect sources, one piece of disillusionment after another that broke and pulverized me. If not for the magistrate's phone call, I would surely have learned the news on the street: it would have been thrown at me point blank without any warning.

I blame that lawyer a lot for what she did to me. I often remember the time we first met. I'm pretty intuitive. I knew right
away whom I was dealing with and I hated her even more for
it. Did she sense this? Was this some kind of revenge? I don't
dare imagine it. Such an attitude would be unworthy of a professional, and of an association that aids children. For months I
waited for a letter of explanation. During that time, I hoped she
would change my attitude toward the justice system by interven-
ing in some way. I was full of illusions. I was nothing for her but
another "dreadful" case sent from the association.

My mother, who never gave up, succeeded in reaching the
woman. She first tried to weasel out of it, then insisted that she
didn't represent me, rather the civil party of the association. She
then added that if we had thought of offering a small honorar-
ium, things could have been different. My mother exploded and
I definitively lost any belief in the justice system.

My bag of hard knocks suddenly weighed a hundred kilos more.
I kept my burden and my hatred to myself, not a word left my
mouth. And anyway, I was incapable of formulating anything in
coherent language. All I could do was return the blows I received.

I was eighteen now. An eighteen-year-old girl should be happy
and carefree. She should be biting into life. But here I was burdened
down, weary of living too many things, sick of life. I didn't exist.
I breathed, that was all. Reading the woman's magazine *Marie-
Claire* one afternoon, I came across an article that talked about
rapes and incest. I ripped out the page where there was an address given for a family psychotherapy center. Maybe my mother
would agree to try it out. It was out of the question for my father, of course. My mother made an appointment and the two of
us went. It was at the Buttes-Chaumont in a quiet, inconspicu-
ous house. The decor was nice, both minimalist and very gentle.
I liked the shrink's style. She had a '60s star quality about her,

with butterfly glasses. She put me at ease, asked me a range of questions. I liked the fact that she didn't mince her words. She seemed to know what was going on in the housing projects and about the gang rapes there. It all convinced me to trust her. I felt hope again. She received my mother separately. I didn't hear what they talked about. I felt content leaving the consultation. A little spark of enthusiasm, a hint of hope, was reignited in me. Maybe I'd found a solution to my problems.

"So what do you think?"

"She seems nice."

"Yeah, I'm glad, because she understands me. She wants me to come once a week to start with. What do you think?"

"You know, Sami . . ."

Right, I see! When she took that tone, I knew what it meant.

"Wait, listen to me, it's three hundred francs a session. It's not reimbursed by social security and she doesn't take additional health insurance."

Why the heck was she talking about social security and health insurance!

"But we have money!"

"Yeah, and? That doesn't mean we should do it!"

I'd stopped listening to her, I'd stopped hearing her. I let her scream.

"It's always the same with you! As soon as someone says no to you, you throw a fit! You sulk like a little child!"

Go on, keep talking! I wasn't listening anymore and I wasn't hearing anymore!

I was devastated by my mother's reaction. I was worth nothing in her eyes. I didn't deserve any effort. I'd forgotten that my mother didn't let go of her cash that easily. However, I knew that if money was lacking at certain times in the past, it was no longer the case. We weren't millionaires, but we could live decently.

18. The Fight

How could I erase it all? I had to keep moving. I looked for work. No way was I going to be a cashier at Carrefour or a cleaning woman. I wanted a gratifying job in a nice environment. I didn't want to spend my days with hassled customers, people stressed from morning till night. Work that required using foreign languages interested me. I was good in English and I still spoke Flemish fluently. Something artistic or craft oriented would have suited me very well: fine arts, theater . . .

I visited the local job center and jotted down all the ads that interested me. That year, I started a series of professional development courses. Initiation to theater, to audiovisual, to drawing. "Preparatory qualification for fine arts," etc.

During an internship I met Térésa, mother of a five-year-old girl named Emma. Térésa changed my life. She was the first person to consider me as an artist. She thought I had talent and liked my way of harmonizing colors. Behind the street punk, she saw a sensitive person, she glimpsed the creative soul. This touched me deeply and reconciled me with myself a little.

A few months later I began a foreign language course, "Mastering English." I wanted to have a profession that allowed me to travel. Artistic professions are swell, but it's hell finding a job! To complete my training, I interned as a hotel receptionist. Goodbye sneakers and jeans, hello suit and high heels! It didn't last long. I felt like an imposter. I got so bored I quit after a month!

I was twenty-years-old and my life was a mess. I tried to act normal, like everyone else, melting into the crowd. I didn't succeed. Told to move on, I moved on, advancing in the jungle called life. I advanced without knowing why, without any goal or desire. I picked up odd jobs: selling clothing or merguez sandwiches at the Clignancourt flea market. I made a huge effort to enter the masquerade. I played my roles, but I wasn't myself. I put a ton of energy into interesting myself in what I did, but my unease always returned full force. It was a vicious circle that built walls around me, walls I was constantly hitting up against. I changed jobs, company, but my inner state never changed. That ball remained lodged in my throat, and the snakes too, squirming in my bag of woes. I didn't succeed in stabilizing myself or concentrating on my work. My social life was miserable. I told anyone I didn't like to take a hike. I laid down my own law, made my own rules, to better protect myself. I heard nothing people told me, I had no professional conscience or skills. I worked to buy dope, period.

At twenty-one years old, I found a secretarial position through relatives. I had regular hours for a year, which permitted me to rent an apartment. It was a cozy one-bedroom in the kind of older building I like, in Saint-Denis. My life with my parents had become intolerable. They constantly threw the same old lines at me: "When are you going to stop dragging your feet?" "That's all in the past!" The more my mother pissed me off with her remarks, the more aggressive I became. I swore at her, threw things, transforming myself into a monster, to the point of scaring her. It was the only way I could find to make her leave me in peace.

One morning, after yet another crisis, she resolved to find me an apartment. She took me to a real estate agency where one of her friends worked. I visited the apartment in the morning, and that afternoon I had the keys. What joy to finally have my own place, four walls to do anything I wanted. I was so sick of other people's homes, I was ecstatic, imagining the best.

Lyes moved in with me. Despite the low blows, I still believed in my relationship with him. I thought moving in together could improve things. I was twenty-one and he was twenty-two. We'd been together for five years and it felt like a lifetime. I quickly learned that living together, for him, meant nothing. He hung with his buddies all day long and only returned to sleep. I discovered the philosophy of Lyes and his friends. The truth was, in his neighborhood, no one went out with his meuf. You went out to bars with "sluts," meufs no one respects. "They'll think I'm a faggot if I go out with my meuf!" So the story went. Under the pretext of being "hyperrespected," I found myself alone at home while mister got his kicks. I got stuck with the shopping, the laundry, the rent. I couldn't even keep him home with little dinners. Lyes's life was outside.

I'd calmed down though, no more partying, no nothing. I didn't ask him where he'd been. I was sure he was cheating on me, although I never caught him. When I tried to express my frustration and my suspicions, he diverted the conversation or reproached me for Mourad and the others. He hassled me, insulted me, guilt-tripped me. In short he twisted everything around. He was a regular salesman, manipulating me all the time. And I bought it, like a moron. More than that, I was convinced I needed his forgiveness! I asked him to leave me or forgive me. He left, but always came back. Why? He told me his presence was his forgiveness. No comment!

One day I learned that Lyes spent his nights smoking and drinking with friends in an apartment belonging to some meufs, two of whom I knew. I showed up and crashed the party. Among the girls, there was Monique, the girl who had saved my life when I overdosed. After losing sight of her for a long time, we became chums again during these evenings. But the mood was weird. Lyes was uncomfortable in my presence. I played the dumb chick, like I didn't see what was going on. Nothing was said, it was all in the looks: I suspected two of the girls there to be hot for Lyes, or to have already slept with him. Since I was a bother, they found a strategy to have fun with me and hurt me in the process.

"Hello, Samira? How's it going, it's Monique!"

"Hey, cool, you?"

"Okay, just dragging a bit with school."

"So what's up?"

"Nothing, just wanted to see how you're doing, and then there's something I wanted to talk to you about."

"Oh, yeah? What's that?"

"You see, there's a rumor going around Saint-Denis. It seems K. is out and he's looking for you!"

Monique knew all about it, because after the hospital episode, I had confided in her. What she just told me was terrifying.

"Oh, really? Who told you that?"

"I can't tell you, I promised I'd keep it secret."

"Well, listen up, you started, you finish!"

"OK! I'll tell you, but I'm not saying who it is."

"Go on!"

"Well, a meuf who knows all about it told me that people had seen K. at the Gare-du-Nord and that he was looking for you—to butcher you! Some say you deserve it 'cause you were asking for it and the only thing that hasn't ridden you is the RER!"

"Oh, yeah? Bring me the slut who said that!"

"It's bad, you gotta watch out. What are you going to do?"

"I'm gonna break that whore's ass who said that, then, I'm gonna call someone who can tell me if K. is really out."

I was so sunk in my nightmare that I jumped with both feet into her stupid trap. I believed her story! She put in all the ingredients: suspense, mystery, and enough drama to seriously feed my fear. She played with my mind, forcing me into a game of "mystery guest" by refusing to give me the names of the people who had spoken.

"You don't know them."

"That's OK, they don't know me either, but that doesn't stop them from talking about me."

"Be careful," she told me, "it's you I'm worried about, I'm your friend." Skank. She kept me running, leading me around for several days. She served me a total mishmash impossible to untangle. Pressed to talk, she cracked in the end and gave me the address of one of the girls talking about me. I told them to meet me in Saint-Denis to clear things up.

A little voice in my head told me not to go alone. Two girlfriends and a guy friend accompanied me in case it got out of hand. That evening, of course, no one showed up. We waited. Getting impatient, I decided to go directly over to one of the girls who were doing all the talking and ring her doorbell. It had been two months they'd been breaking my balls to make me scared, dragging me around from one storyteller to the next. That evening, I was determined to resolve the situation and force those wagging tongues to spit it up. The girl whose door I rang at put on a whole show. She told me she was having troubles with her guy. He had kicked her out three months ago and, it just so happened, that night she wanted to go collect her clothes, her curtains, and her dish towels. It smelled fishy right away, it was written on her fleeing look.

"I'm having a fight with Vidad, he's throwing everything out the window, I have to go!"

She laid a whole sob story on me there.

"Oh, yeah? Well, we're going with you! Just in case you get in a fight! That way we can resolve this thing right after. 'Cause I'm not leaving, dig it? As long as this thing ain't resolved, I'm not leaving!"

Her face turned white. She was not happy, she had thought she could get rid of me with her two-bit story. We all headed off to her homeboy's place, which was fifty yards down the block. Turned out he was Monique's brother. Small world!

Arriving at the apartment building, I saw that everything was calm and nothing had been thrown out the window. She rang the intercom to go up. We waited below smoking a little joint and talking quietly. After fifteen minutes I heard calls for help on the intercom and I recognized the slut's voice. I went up with my guy friend to see what was happening and help her out if need be.

Entering the apartment, I picked up a knife off the floor and hid it behind my back. No way did I have any trust in that skank. When I entered the living room, the spectacle I saw there was surreal, a real banlieue vaudeville act. There was Monique's brother's new meuf hiding under the table, screaming. Monique's brother was slapping his "ex" around, the blabbering bitch. She in turn was gripping her dish towels howling "Help!" while her brother, who arrived out of nowhere, distractedly tried to separate the two "exes." A regular madhouse! I would have loved to laugh hysterically, but it wasn't exactly the moment.

I had the clear impression that it was pure theater, because there was a total lack of conviction. What this bitch was ready to do to avoid explaining herself! I intervened anyway, you never knew.

"Hey! Let her go! What do you think you're doing?" I said in my big street voice.

"What the hell are you doing in my home, scram!" replied Monique's brother.

"Oh, shut up! Either you let her go or I'll slash your face with this knife! And you, little fag, your sister is getting beaten up and you barely move! What the hell is this madhouse?"

Right then, the brother-in-law lost it and pointed a gun at me. I wondered what my friend was doing and just why he was there. It'd been a half hour since I'd seen him! I'd known the brother-in-law for a long time, even before he had married Monique's sister. The hoods in the banlieue are like a bunch of small towns, we all know each other.

"Hey, Bachir! It's me, don't you recognize me?"

"I don't give a flying fuck! Beat it!"

The gun pointed at me was pretty persuasive and I didn't insist. I delicately laid the knife on the floor, making sure he saw me. I stepped backward out of the apartment, but not without lancing a threat at that fat bitch: "I'm not forgetting you, I'll be waiting below, I got the whole night!"

I wanted to finish with this thing tonight. The next act arrived: Monique, accompanied by her parents. At first I didn't see her parents, they held back to see what I was going to do. Nasty! She advanced all alone toward me, to go upstairs.

"So, Monique, you missed our meeting? But that's no prob, you know, I've got the whole evening to fuck with you, you stupid bitch!"

"You got a problem, you little hussy?"

It was Monique's father who had just addressed me. He lifted his T-shirt to show me the handgun he was packing between his huge gut and his pants.

"Aha, we're all packing tonight! Okay, you win this time! But you see, I'm not moving! Bring anyone you want, I'm not moving! On my mother's grave, I'm not moving, you dirty slut!"

That was enough for Monique, who started moving toward the doors of the building.

"We're calling the cops on you and then we'll see if you don't get moving, you piece of trash!" the father called to me, following his wife and daughter into the building.

"Call them, I'll tell them what you've got under your shirt, asshole!"

I had no intention of moving. There was something weird about this whole scene. That was what convinced me to stay down below. I saw them all observe me from their windows. Soon as I lifted my head, they hid.

Ten minutes later a band of about a dozen homeboys showed up. Apparently, Monique had called the posse. Unlucky for her, because I knew all of them: we were old schoolmates.

"Sup, yo! Been a long time! How's it going?"

"Just chilling."

"There's a ho called me up, got some kind of trouble up here! It's not with you by any chance?"

Monique was really starting to squeeze me, to draw a crowd even from her hiding place! While my friend talked with one of the homeboys, I discretely asked one of my girlfriends to go to the project to get my cousin and his friends. I also asked her to warn my mother. Since Monique had brought her parents along, it'd be fairer. To each her adult!

I picked up the conversation with the homeboys. It was clear they had no desire to quarrel with me, especially when I explained the reason for my presence.

"But this thing went down a long time ago! It's been five, six years now, right?"

"Sure has! But there are stupid sluts who like to gossip. They gossip even though I didn't know them back then. They've been breaking my balls for two months with this thing! At first I just wanted them to fess up, but now she's brought you into it, I'm going to kill them both!"

If she thought she could intimidate me with her ten homeboys, she was going to be surprised by what happened! My cousin arrived and not with ten dudes, but a whole mob. There were guys from three different projects. In no time there were about forty of them hanging outside the building. I yelled into the intercom, "You slut, you wanted a posse, look out the window!"

I filled my cousin in on what was happening, without mentioning the guns. I didn't want things to unravel and him to get shot. I was a little worried about how the evening would turn out. There was a whole tribe of people milling around the building entrance now. No one really wanted a fight. The mood was more wanting to understand what was happening.

"But I thought you were robbing the apartment!"

"Oh, yeah? You heard that? That bitch can really cook it up! I came to get an explanation for the rumors she and her girlfriends have been spreading about me to make me scared. When I arrived, her brother-in-law and her faggot father flashed their guns on me. Then she got a whole band of homeboys to descend on me. Now you're telling me I wanted to rob her apartment, it's too much! That bitch has no fear!"

Monique had told everyone that I was trying to break into her brother's apartment so her gang would intervene and beat me up. That also explained the presence of her father and his piece. I

141

was nauseated by such vileness, such gratuitous nastiness. What had I done to her to make her want to hurt me this much?

My mother arrived at that moment. She was fuming because she'd been hearing about this business with Monique for two months.

"Who's breaking my daughter's balls here, huh?"

She scared us, we hadn't seen her arrive. She confronted all the young people there.

"It wasn't me, ma'am!"

"It wasn't me, ma'am!"

My cousin took advantage of the confusion on the sidewalk to run into the building and up to the floor where they were all barricaded.

"Hey! Your cousin is up there!"

"Shit! He shouldn't be up there, they have guns!"

My mother decided to go up too, to have a talk with Monique's parents and calm my cousin down. I didn't feel like going up. I had no desire to tell my story, the rapes, etc. How humiliating! All I wanted was to destroy the little rat faces of those two bitches hiding up there!

Through the intercom, my mother asked me to go up. When I got up there, the hallway was full of people, but it was as silent as a graveyard. Everyone was listening to my mother as she spoke about me, about my life, about the suffering I'd carried around all these years. No one dared interrupt her. I was astounded. I had never heard her speak like this about me, using the words "rape" and "suffering." It was the first time she had defended me. I was so surprised to hear what she thought of me, and so touched by what she was doing, that I felt like crying. Suddenly, I lost all desire to beat up those jerks.

"Monique has been calling Sam on the phone for over two months, claiming her attacker is out of prison, that she should be on her guard. And that's not the least of it! She's playing with her nerves and her suffering! Honestly, I do not wish on your daughter what happened to mine!"

Man, my mother had really fooled me! I was totally blown away.

"Listen, ma'am, we weren't aware of all this. We thought the girl was coming with her gang to trash the place. We're terribly sorry!"

Monique's mother walked toward her daughter and delivered a hard slap in the face.

"I knew you were a little shit, but this tops it all! From now on, you're not putting one foot outside. We'll deal with this at home!"

The situation ended there for everybody concerned except me. It was the first time I felt such a tenacious rancor toward someone. I swore to myself that I would smash in that slut's face no matter the place or moment or however long it took. She never completely left my thoughts, and everywhere I went, I looked for her. The opportunity presented itself three years later. I bumped into Monique while shopping for groceries at Carrefour. I was in the canned peas and carrots aisle when I spied her. Calmly, I parked my cart and approached her.

"Sup, Monique?"

"Hey, not much! Nice to see you again!" she said to me with a big smile.

What a bullshit artist.

"Oh, yeah? You ask me how I am with a big smile like that! You got a short memory!"

She didn't have time to respond before I punched her in the head.

"Remember that fight?"

"But it wasn't me, it was my brother, he was . . ."

I didn't let her finish. She got another punch in the head.

"Oh! Now it's your brother! Why not your grandmother too!"

Bam! My fists were flying. I smashed her nose where she was already bleeding. To finish her off, I threw a wad of spit in her face. I was about to leave when she yelled back, "That's not the end of this!"

Oh yeah? Very calmly, I turned back, taking up a can of peas and carrots along the way. Still calm, I told her, "Listen up, you piece of shit! Bring whoever you want: your whole family, all the people living in this city if that makes you happy, I don't give a flying fuck! Is that clear? I'm gonna burn your family, fuck them up one by one! And this one is for being such a loudmouth!" Bam! She got the can of peas and carrots right in her nose. She was pissing blood. I had no interest in hanging around too long there, or I'd end up with the cops. I calmly returned to my red shopping cart to blend in and headed toward the check-out area.

Damn! I was trembling all over, my legs barely held me up, and my heart was beating a mile a minute. I also had a big bump on my forehead from two punches she gave me. I pretended to examine my groceries while checking to look around. I have to admit, I had shown her no mercy. I'd destroyed her rat face. She really did have the face of a rat, the little dark round eyes, pointed snub nose, and teeth of a rodent. A real rat head. I'd just given her a free facial reconstruction. She should have thanked me!

"Excuse me, were you the one who hit that young lady there?"

Shit, security! I hadn't seen him approach me. Well, what did I have to lose!

"Yup, it was me. I'm really sorry that had to happen here at Carrefour, sir. That girl sent a bunch of boys to me two years ago to beat me up. I ended up in the hospital for two weeks. I swore to myself that if I ever found her again, I'd get back at her! I just saw her and I got back at her!"

"But you've destroyed her face!"

"You should have seen mine two years ago!"

The security guard understood that it was a settling of scores between meufs. He had no wish to get involved. He even smiled, nodding. Apparently two meufs fighting made him chuckle.

"You're a high-strung one, aren't you! OK, OK, hurry up and check out."

"Thank you, sir, yup, I'll hurry up."

Phew! What luck! It was hard to believe! True, she could have still filed a complaint and sent the cops after me.

Two days later I happened to run into her on a bus. She was hiding behind dark sunglasses, but her face was a regular rainbow of colors. It went from blue to yellow to mauve to dark purple! It was actually hard to recognize her. Passing by her, I couldn't stop myself from whispering a little warning, "Lower your eyes or I'll do it again!" I then went to sit near the exit door so I could watch once again before she got off the bus. I savored my vengeance and my "superior force." But it was kind of hollow; deep down, I was not very proud of myself. The aggressiveness I felt scared me. I knew I was only obeying the law of the projects, which demands we defend our reputations an eye for an eye. I definitely would have used my intelligence sooner than my aggressiveness if all this Machiavellian murkiness, all the threats and gossip, had not pushed me to the limit. I was also hurt, I admit, by Lyes's lack of support. I should have known by now—he'd proven it enough—that I couldn't expect anything from him. But this whole affair was because of him. Monique had tried to hit on him one evening, and when it didn't work, she took it out on me. Lyes preferred to remain neutral, claiming it was a fight between meufs and that I was imagining things! I later learned that Monique also hated me because she couldn't stand me being such good friends with Fabrice, her boyfriend at the time.

Lyes tried my patience to the limits, wasting away the dwindling reserve of my affection for him. He took no account of what had happened and refused all dialogue. He didn't want to hear that I felt spurned by his lack of involvement. According to him, I was imagining it all and this whole problem with Monique was just a crazy thing between girls. He was so adamant, he made me doubt myself. This affair forced me to change my attitude toward him. I kept bringing it up. It was a daily war. I acted like my mother with me, employing the same tactics. I tyrannized him continually. So he took more and more space. He disappeared now for weeks at a time, claiming he was at raves. . . . Seriously, he just took me for one long ride!

19. Grilled

After my stint as a secretary, I stayed on unemployment for a few months until I found a job training program that really grabbed me: games and activity leader at a holiday resort. It was right up my alley—fluency in a foreign language, training in dance, singing, acting, and drawing. I was chosen for the training session and spent six months learning all the secrets of resort activities, while having a blast doing it. It included everything from group games like lotto or bingo to evening theatrical events, with inside info on the secrets of personal relations with clients, ballroom dancing, choreographies, sketches, archery, etc. The complete palette of a successful resort professional.

My teacher, Sabrina, believed in me and gave me a lot of encouragement. She had a weak spot for me and closed her eyes to my failings, my lack of punctuality, for example. She helped discover my acting talents and mirrored back a very positive self-image. It gave me a break from the image of "street scum" I usually carried around.

Then an unexpected, unimaginable, fabulous thing happened. Our group was chosen to play Petronius's *Satiricon* at the Trévise Theater in Paris. We played with costumes and masks, and worked on gesture and mime. A total blast. I learned how to put on a real show with scenery, lighting, costumes . . . I was flying so high I never noticed the time go by. I'd get home and drop, exhausted. Two months earlier I'd been loafing; today I was running nonstop. Training courses all day, two shows at the theater every evening. There was no more time to sink into depression over Lyes. I forgot about him thanks to friends I made at the theater. I discovered what it meant to be part of a group, the moments of hysterical laughter during rehearsal. It was a powerful experience, a dream come true. I had never experienced so many positive things, I couldn't quite believe it was real.

One night we all went for a night cap in a Karaoke bar near the Paris Opera. It was the first evening I didn't feel scared going out. To the contrary, I felt carefree and happy. I was with warm-hearted, healthy people. It was another world altogether and I felt at home in it. I had my own friends, a little band of crazy nuts a lot like me. Toward the end of the evening, I invited those who didn't live in Paris to crash at my place. Anita, Fatou, Abdel, and Yanis accepted. We'd spent a good evening and were feeling particularly high. Carrying on our conversation, we rolled a few joints. Anita and Fatou fell asleep in no time. That left me talking with Abdel and Yanis. Abdel, who was twenty-five and came from Lille, didn't have the ghetto mentality: he was open and funny. It was a pleasure to talk with him. Yanis was eighteen and he was the pretty boy of the group. Before beginning the training program, he had played soccer on the Paris-Saint-Germain juniors team. He'd had to stop his career due to a knee injury. He was a real charmer and flirted with all the meufs in the group. He tried it on me, but I quickly told him to take a hike. I couldn't take him seriously when I saw him putting on a show for everyone. That evening, however, I caught several side glances, although I didn't immediately understand what they meant.

Anita was asleep next to Abdel and Fatou had taken the couch. They were fast asleep and I didn't want to wake them. Only one solution was left: I'd share my bed with Yanis. I made things clear:

"Look, you stay on your side, got it?"

I suspected Yanis and Abdel of setting this little trap. I was ready for anything, except for what Yanis whispered.

"I don't know how to start . . . I want to explain . . . I know I got to be straight with you. . . . It's hard to talk to you, you really intimidate me."

"C'mon, Yanis, don't start with that!"

"Hey, to me, you're the only star up there on stage! I know I'm just a kid in your eyes, I'm only eighteen!"

"And your pretty boy number with the stage meufs, what's that about? You take me for a twit? Go on, get out of here, you can't fool me!"

"I really have to lay it out for you, don't I? It's you I want to get to know. When you're acting, I'm like a crazy man, I can't keep my eyes off you. Let me prove I'm not just a kid! Anyway, who cares about our age difference? I'm being up front with you, Sam. I love everything about you. Your smile, your eyes, your hair. Man, your eyes kill me! And your personality! I love everything about you, Sam!"

"Yanis, my life is way too complicated. . . . Look, I'll think it over, but now, let's just sleep. Okay?"

"Listen, Sam, I'm not a jerk. Believe me!"

Whoa! I'd never heard one of those before, a real declaration of love, like in the movies! I was impressed, I was taken aback. For someone who was used to the manners and speech of animals, this tenderness threw me for a loop.

All the little rich chicks in the training program ran after him and Sam the street punk was the one he preferred! I couldn't believe I aroused such feelings.

It'd been over two months since I'd seen Lyes. I didn't feel like gluing the pieces together again. I was tired, worn down by what he brought into my life. I was tired of the suffering, of waiting for something that would never come. I knew he wouldn't change. His life was all about having fun with his buddies, throwing his money away. I didn't want to spend my life waiting for a man with the fear he'd get thrown in the slammer sooner or later. I didn't want to be home cooking up the couscous while he was out living his life. I didn't want to raise kids in this rotten hood. I didn't want to reproduce what my mother had done twenty years earlier.

I realized this while hanging out with Yasmine, Lydie, and Sandrine. Yasmine was the mother of an adorable, little mixed-race child, Shana. Sandrine was a couple of months pregnant. All four of us were suckers in love. We ran after men who ran after money. We spent our time looking for them, wondering what they were doing, and with whom. Evenings, when they deigned to come home, we had no right to complain, which meant endless fights. Because of love, we accepted this situation, we submitted to it, we stayed.

In this dump of a hood, the guys were all made from the same mold. Lyes was typical of them. The "good guys" were exceptions. Yasmine's and Sandrine's boyfriends were in the slammer for gang rape. They were in an apartment with a "slut," as they put it, a girl who turned them on and they couldn't resist. . . . Like how! I knew that tune!

I used to talk, joke, share nice moments with those guys and it turned out they were capable of raping a girl and blaming her for their actions. It was disgusting. Who could you trust? I didn't want to share my thoughts with Yasmine and Sandrine. In any case they were convinced of their boyfriends' innocence. They didn't ask questions. It wasn't their fault, the girl was asking for it! They only thought of one thing—getting those assholes out of prison—and they spent a crazy amount of time working on that. One pregnant, the other with a baby girl. They worked overtime to pay for lawyers and sent money orders every week to cover those gentlemen's expenses. Two times a week they'd make the long commute for visiting hours. They had to trek to the local equivalent of Bab el-Oued City, with baby carriages and bags full of laundry, filled with dirty clothes on the return trip, and the kids. They had to send their guys mail, upbeat if possible, to keep their little morales up. If not, everyone pulled a long face at the visiting room. It was pure hell.

I'm not saying life in prison is all roses, but the people who carry and morally and financially support prisoners are their wives. When their men are in the joint, women literally scrape the floors to get by. They lose their liberty too. They take care of everything: pregnancies, births, the education of the children, food, rent, fees, lawyers. They run around like madwomen trying to repair the stupid mistakes made by their men. Sandrine and Yasmine reminded me of my mother, and when I saw little Shana, I saw myself as a child. It was the same story. I had no frigging desire for that kind of life. I didn't want some guy who was in and out of prison. I didn't want to run after lawyers. I didn't want the Sunday face-offs during visiting hours, with the kids bouncing on my knee. I refused to get caught in the whirlpool that sucks in women like Sandrine and Yasmine for life.

What I wanted was a normal guy, one who came home at night, talked to me, found me pretty, showed interest in his kids' education. A normal guy, you know! They existed, didn't they?

I wanted to forget where I came from, to start a new life. Lyes would never escape the treadmill he was caught on. He was playing with fire, with his life, pushing everything to the limit. His motto constantly led him on: "Fuck others before they fuck you over." I was not going to be a part of that game. I was sick of living a life of tears. I wanted to meet interesting people who respected me and who would help me grow up, people who would bring beauty into my life.

Evenings, in character behind his mask, Yanis's eyes followed me everywhere. He sent me silent cries of "I love you!" and I received them bashfully. During the day he was full of attention for me, kind, funny, charming. His maturity made me forget his age. I'd never known these feelings. I was bathed in tenderness and love and it scared me. It was all too good for someone like me. At any moment I expected to be hit with something along the lines of, "I really hooked that hard-ass!" or "Ha, ha, I was just joking!"

I was scared of contaminating the beauty, health, and kindness I saw in Yanis. I came from a dark, filthy, vicious world. I was also afraid of Lyes. I was his meuf, his possession in other words, and he wouldn't let me go so easily. It hadn't been said out loud, but it was sufficiently understood. One night, after the show, I decided to believe Yanis and throw myself blindly into the open arms of possibility. I invited him to spend the night with me, hoping that Lyes wouldn't have the ill-timed presumption to show up that same evening after a three-month absence.

My life became pure joy after that night spent together. Every day Yanis smothered me in love. I discovered magnificent emotions that swept away the nightmarish years with Lyes in one stroke. I forgot everything in Yanis's arms. With him I was a beautiful woman, even while I slept. I woke up to breakfast in bed, tender kisses, bouquets of roses. He took me out to restaurants and under my napkin I sometimes found surprise gifts.

With him life smiled at me big time. At the theater, we had found a hiding place to meet before the show. In a small corner unknown to everyone the fire raged. We were consumed with desire to talk, touch, feel, embrace. We promised to never leave each other again. The happiness I felt raised questions about my relationship with Lyes—had we ever loved each other? What tied us together? How could I have stayed so long in a loveless relationship with him?

One night Karima, one of the interns, gave me, Fatou, and Yanis a lift. In the back seat Yanis wrapped himself around me as we listened to music and I distractedly gazed out the window at the cars on the Périphérique. All of a sudden, in a car alongside us, I recognized Lyes with his buddies. He turned his head in my direction and recognized me. He started to beep like a madman, apparently enraged, and I read his lips: "I gotcha! I gotcha!" He held me in his gaze and slid his thumb across his throat. It's the gesture of throat cutting, which back home we call "the Berber smile." It sent a chill up my spine. Karima stepped on the gas and lost him on the beltway.

From that day on, my peace of mind was shot. I discovered him hanging around the theater, I received anonymous phone calls, and I kept watch wherever I went. I was determined, however, to never see him again, and he sensed it.

Yanis and I had to end our tender love story. When the play ended, we would all scatter to different corners of the world to complete our on-site training. I didn't dare imagine the after-Yanis period, I took full advantage of the moments that remained. He promised he wouldn't forget me, that he'd write and call me every day. He made long-term projects and talked about what we'd do when we got back from our three-month internships. I smiled but kept silent. He spoke with the enthusiasm of his eighteen years and didn't realize that what we'd experience would transform us. Three months wasn't much, but it could mean a lifetime.

My internship took place in the Savoie, in Saint-Jean-de-Maurienne. Les Carlines was a hotel-resort with a family ambiance. I loved it. The team was super; the director, Michèle, was warm-hearted, competent, and funny. I learned a lot with her. During the day, we fixed costumes and scenery for the evening sketches or spent time rehearsing. Sometimes we joined the clients for drinks on the slopes, disguised as pirates. Twice a week there was a theme dinner, anything from beach or oriental night to alien or vampire banquet. Then we'd have to decorate the dining hall, coming up with fresh ideas for scenery, and make and paint them on the spot. For the alpine climber evening, I ended up hanging from the restaurant ceiling, suspended in a harness. . . .

We created shows from scratch. We improvised sketches and indulged in unforgettable laughing fits. Fred, Stephan, and I were always ready to clown around on stage and propose crazy scenes that cracked up Michèle and the group. There was a real, rare fusion among us all. On the client side it was also a pleasure, some said my smile and my kindness made their vacations. It gave me a funny feeling, as if they were talking about someone else. The only false note—excuse the pun—was the karaoke nights. I sang about as good as a broken violin, so those evenings Michèle let me have a night off!

I preferred helping out in the bar, which avoided my having to loaf in my room rereading Yanis's letters. He was in Kenya, a killer location for practical training. He woke up dangling his feet in turquoise-colored water teaming with multicolored fish. But he was bored, the hotel had few guests and most of them were on the old side. For activities, there wasn't much to plan. He had plenty of free time to dream about me and send me marvelously passionate, perfumed letters, which were joyously transporting. I couldn't get over being loved like this, an experience so new. His presence in my life was like touching the moon! Yet deep down, a little voice remained vigilant: "He's only eighteen, Sam! At that age, love doesn't last for the rest of your life! Take care!" I'd begun to understand life now, and I didn't give much weight to big promises anymore. With his charm and his talent, Yanis was sure to be sought after; for him, things could change in an instant.

When I got back from the internship, I learned that we were leaving for a new destination. I was heading to Greece, Yanis was off to Crete. We celebrated our lovers' reunion at my place, but something was different. Yanis had changed, he'd become distant. Now he saw everything through the eyes of his mentor in Kenya, a guy who'd become his best buddy. This great mentor made a very bad impression on me. A real talker, and unscrupulous, he hid a nasty streak behind a fast-paced facade. I sensed cocaine was what was holding him together. I was careful not to say anything about this to Yanis, it wouldn't have done any good, he was too sunk in this thing. Our paths parted, such had been our understanding. "Each his own direction, each his own path." We each had a job, selling smiles to tourists. We parted in Athens, he on a plane to Crete and I on a bus to a hotel forty kilometers from the capital. Taking leave from him, I sobbed on his shoulder like a little girl. During the bus ride, I cried till my head throbbed. Welcome to Greece!

Those last few months had given me valuable experiences and

I gained tremendously from the troupe. My teachers, especially Sabrina, had supported me one hundred percent. In spite of this, and although it was pretty contradictory, I continued to trail my bag of woes and fall into seizures. I continued to blow up at the slightest emotion. It was like I wanted people to know I was brimming with pain. "Hey!" my fits insisted, "I'm pain personified and I want you all to get it loud and clear!" I felt pathetic about these repetitive discharges, but I couldn't help them. I had to explode. I didn't realize the toll this was taking on my work. They started to hesitate to send me out during vacation season. Sabrina insisted I should be given a chance. She believed in me, which did me a load of good.

In Greece we worked round the clock. During the day we ran activities, and at night we prepared and rehearsed shows. I loved this hectic rhythm, but I couldn't hold up. I was overextended and this translated into more seizures. They became worse and worse, and happened with more frequency. I tried to hold up with all my strength, but I was too shattered. The director wanted to send me back to Paris, but Sabrina suggested a small hotel in Cyprus where the work was light.

The hotel had a very small crew. There was Lucien, the activities coordinator, and me. Later, he added his meuf and two interns. The atmosphere was not so hot. An ex-commando sergeant, Lucien still believed he was in the army. He yelled all the time and didn't give a damn. We tried to organize activities with what was at hand. His meuf had no talents and no experience in sports, activities, or theater, and the two interns thought they were on vacation. Result: I did everything.

After four months at that rhythm, I was working as hard as I could, but I was often down in the dumps. I wanted to prove that I could do the whole season. We had a few perks, including a scooter, which gave me the opportunity to escape. I saw friends or spent the afternoon at the beach. Sometimes I left with Aziz, one of the interns. He was a rascal, that one. Didn't lift a finger but always managed to turn a quick one. I went clothes shopping with him sometimes. We visited all the chic stores. He didn't skimp, Aziz, even offered me a pair of Timberland boots. Generous, huh! At the time I didn't raise an eyebrow.

Days came and went, and the clients too. My craving for a joint grew, the mood definitely soured. After a big chat, I managed to get three days in Paris and I brought back some pot. In Paris I met up with Lyes, who was ready to try anything to get some dough. He was like a madman when he was broke. I'd never seen him so desperate. I also sensed that my departure hadn't left him indifferent. His way of showing it was to put his hands up my skirt. Such a romantic!

Back in Cyprus I returned to loudmouth Lucien and his moron of a girlfriend. Some nights, after work, I fixed a fruit salad with stuff I'd bought from a kind old Cypriot. I'd sit out on the terrace to enjoy it and smoke a joint. Gazing up, I talked to the stars. I asked them to help me end out the season. In my fog, I had the impression they answered me by twinkling a little brighter and I felt reassured.

One afternoon, after an aquatic bodybuilding class, I got ready to leave for a ride on my scooter. The receptionist called out to me and told me two men wanted to speak to me in the manager's office. There I found Lucien, Aziz, and two muscle men with thick moustaches. They asked me to confirm my identity, which I did.

I found out they were plainclothes Cypriot cops. Without a word, they gestured for me and Aziz to follow them. They took us to a police station in Aya Napa. Usually I went to Aya Napa to dance but I figured this time I'd find only thick moustaches, the Greek version of *Midnight Express*. When they spoke Greek, it sounded like they were constantly bickering. It was quite impressive. I couldn't figure out a word they were saying. I sweat bullets on a bench for eight hours with no idea what I was there for. I started to panic.

The precinct captain also looked the part, and his mug made me flip out. He asked a ton of questions in English with his crazy accent. You had to concentrate to understand. He asked me if I knew Aziz and whether he was my boyfriend, whether I slept with him, went shopping with him, etc. I quickly understood that the shoes and two T-shirts Aziz had given me were bought with a credit card stolen from a hotel not far from ours. He'd charged over thirty thousand francs! For clothes! Shit, the loser just couldn't help himself! They picked me up because in some of the security videos I was seen accompanying him on his buying sprees.

For an entire week Midnight Express and his colleagues interrogated me about this stolen credit card, confronting us with each other from time to time. I explained that I didn't know the card was stolen and that Aziz had told me he had a big unemployment check that had been delayed. I told them he wanted to have fun and that once or twice, when I was with him, he offered me some small presents. And all that in English, mind you!

By the evening of the eighth day, they let us go. I wasn't sure what Aziz had told the cops, what pirouette he'd managed to perform, but in any case we were out with orders to return the stolen items by the next day. Midnight Express, with his barreling *R*s in English, warned me to stay away from Aziz. Leaving the station, I saw that Aziz couldn't care less about this whole affair. It was obviously not his first time. But I let him know he had put me in a serious mess.

"Oh, stop bitching! You're out, aren't you? I took all the blame."

"Yeah, maybe, but I had to spend eight days waiting around

for that! And how's it going to look at work, have you thought of that?"

"Yeah, yeah! Don't be a jerk! You're not going to tell me you never snatched a card in Saint-Denis!"

"Fuck off, bastard!"

Damn, let it go, that guy would make me nuts! Luckily for him I was from the same hood. I could have let him drown, but we were in Cyprus, and it was not a place for joking around! If you got the slammer for a joint of marijuana, what was the rap for a stolen credit card?

I ran rings round the cops who tested me to see if I was telling the truth. It allowed me to use the criminal mind I'd acquired. Sam the street scum, though innocent, gave them the runaround. You'd have thought I was the accomplice of a nuclear arms thief! Apparently, they must have enjoyed my company to keep me for eight days. They must get bored stiff at Aya Napa!

I was furious at Aziz, but I didn't say anything to that dumb, egotistic jackass. He didn't even get it. The kid must have been tripping. Thought he pulled one over on them and took himself for a shark, the jerk! He had wrecked everything, my job as events organizer, my plans for the future, my efforts to succeed. He brought me back to zero. What a poor schmuck I was!

Back at the hotel it was worse than I'd imagined. There'd been a leak and the whole hotel knew, clients as well as personnel. Some looked on me as a thief, others asked if I was OK. I shrunk back and focused only on my work. I dared not go out at night. I stayed in my room and smoked. The other intern left, unable to stomach Lucien, who together with his meuf cared only that I did my work. Aziz loafed around and Lucien didn't dare say a thing. Barely a week went by and there was a complete replay: arrest at the hotel, apartment searched, and a second interrogation down at the police station with Sergeant Bushy Moustache.

As it turned out, Aziz had stolen two credit cards. The second one had just now shown up. The debt: twenty thousand francs. Midnight Express put on a big show. He pulled out the list of store purchases, a translator, and a little wooden bat he liked to rhythmically slam into his palm. We were off again!

"Who stole the carrrd?" (That damn R again!)

"Not me!" (I said in English of course.)

"Why didn't you tell me he had another card?"

"I didn't know!"

"But you were with him during his buying sprees!"

"So? I go shopping every day, like I told you already. I go for a walk during my break. I brought you everything back: a pair of shoes. The two T-shirts must have appeared on a different card. Look at the list!"

"Don't tell me how to do my job! Anyway, that's not why I summoned you here."

He began to stare at me for a long time with a twisted look. After a while he said:

"Who does the "hakik" belong to that I found in your room?"

Damn him! He had found a frigging crumb of a bag of weed, a miniscule bud, a stick. Not even enough to roll a joint. I'd been afraid of this when I found out they had a search warrant, but I figured they wouldn't hound me for a piece of shit the size of a rabbit dropping.

"I don't know, I don't smoke!"

I also knew that in Cyprus, as in Crete, the cops didn't get into details with tourists who smoked pot, it was straight to prison with them. Or rather the dungeon! Luckily, they didn't do a house search the first time, I hadn't yet smoked everything. But Midnight Express was now launched into a full-scale live performance. So, no question, whatever happened, I'd have to deny it. That was clear!

After hassling me for two days about the second stolen credit card, he passed on to the "hakik." Who did it belong to? I got an idea. I told him I recalled going out with an English guy I had met at a dance club in Aya Napa. I added that he had spent the night at my place. I called him Bryan, the first name I ever learned in English class!

Go find Bryan, an English pot-smoking tourist! They were everywhere there! The Bryan I knew, in any case, had flown back home to London ages ago. I had to admit that I was pretty proud of my imagination. I passed myself off as a poor dimwit, jilted by a tourist, who found herself arrested for his crime! My snow job worked. Midnight Express took me for a sad meuf. He told me, "Yes, yes, you're right! He fuck you two times!" Yeah, yeah, you're right, you loser! What you're saying is real sweet, but I didn't give a damn, I only wanted to get out of here.

On the sixth day they let me go, but they held on to Aziz. I saw him in the office, all black-and-blue, which surprised me, but I didn't really give a damn. Penniless, I left the police station and hiked twenty kilometers under a leaden sun back to the hotel. I walked like someone enraged, talking to myself, insulting the universe as I kicked at piles of stones along the way. There wasn't a tree to be seen, not a sliver of shade in that godforsaken place. I was bursting with fury. I needed to calm down before I got to the hotel. Twenty kilometers would do the job! They gave me time to think and analyze what awaited me. In any case, right from the start, Lucien had taken me for street scum because of my Beur origins. "The Arabs came to fuck our meufs and steal our jobs!" He was always saying that. Now he'd be happy! Well, there was still no need to exaggerate. I was no Pablo Escobar!

At the hotel, Lucien, the tour operator coordinator, and the hotel manager all greeted me to "thank me for my services." I had expected them to put a quick end to my contract because of the weed, but not to treat me like a dog. They not only fired me, but they also demanded I return the keys to the apartment and use my salary to reimburse part of the credit card debt and pay my return ticket.

I didn't feel like arguing with them because of the problems I had caused them with the weed. I decided to stay silent and accept what happened. I was used to getting blamed and taken for street scum. I was used to injustice. History was repeating itself once again. It reminded me of the trial. I was a victim and I was treated as the criminal. Why should I defend myself when they'd already made up their minds? I found myself in Cyprus without a penny or a roof, alone and in trouble. It broke my heart.

Luckily, Erwin, a hotel client with whom I'd smoked two or three joints and once gotten royally drunk, insisted on helping me. He suggested I sleep in his room without his parents knowing. I was there for less than half an hour when the manager came and threw me out of the room and forbade me access to the hotel. I felt deeply humiliated to be treated this way. They had all forgotten the five months of good work I'd put in. A strong feeling of injustice grabbed me by the throat. I ended up sleeping on the beach. Erwin brought out covers from the hotel so I wouldn't be too cold. He also brought me food. But I was scared of sleeping on the beach. I hadn't forgotten my nightmare in Algeria. I forced myself to stay awake despite my fatigue. I spent the nights begging God to come to my aid and keep me safe on the beach.

Erwin lent me money to call my mother. She was working in Greece and it was not easy to reach her across the language barriers and work schedule problems. After a few days I managed to track her down. She threw her full weight into trying to clear up the mess. She called Sabrina in Paris and threw a fit on the phone. Then, having obtained the phone number of the tour coordinator, she threw another fit. There was plenty to go around! She lectured them about the indecency of treating people in that way. She also had the smarts to remind them I was epileptic and that they needed to think about their responsibility. I swear, my mother would have made an excellent attorney!

That same evening, I moved back into the apartment and the next day I had a return ticket for Paris waiting for me at Larnaca Airport. They also returned my passport, which they'd confiscated. They took a lot out of my salary, which galled me. They left me five hundred francs for my taxi in Paris. What luxury! On top of that they made it understood that I had to pay the rest back when I got to Paris. I was up shit's creek and they just laughed, piling it on.

I got back in a state of shock, totally gutted, blown away by this revolting experience. For two weeks I didn't leave home. I felt beaten down, mortified, sickened that they had taken me for a thief, treated me like dirt, and didn't have the slightest regard for the quality of my work. I also knew where all this was leading: resort activity was finished for me, I was history.

At the same time, I realize today that I accepted unacceptable things there. I acted like a guilty person. How could I have put up with being fired from the hotel like a piece of filth, thrown into the street with my apartment keys, my money, and my passport all confiscated? Why didn't I fight to proclaim my innocence? What was I guilty of? Possessing a small bag of pot. That was all. I behaved like a stray dog who accepts getting kicked in the butt because he's never known anything else and believes he deserves it.

This failure was an enormous disappointment for me. I was born for this profession, I took to it like a fish in water. I had finally found my path and felt happy and appreciated. . . . Talk about being at the wrong place at the wrong time. My hopes were dashed, my life collapsed once again.

20. Insaf, Barry . . .

Well, there I was, rock bottom. All those years I'd managed to keep my head above water. Sure, I'd had to swim against the current, but I kept afloat. I tried with all my strength and soul to keep from drowning. I hung onto reefs dotting this black ocean of a life. Today my life was a total shipwreck. I didn't want to fight for survival anymore. The only desire I had was to sink right under.

I gave in to my tears. My suffering was overwhelming, I couldn't contain it anymore. It overflowed, spilling over onto everything around me.

I stopped going out, I stopped eating, I stopped sleeping. I couldn't make the effort to smile anymore, to make appearances, to bear up, I'd done it too much. I was sick of making efforts to make an effort. I never wanted to hear the phrase "you've got to move on" again. It exhausted me. If I heard "unemployment, social security, job search, rent" one more time, I was ready to take out a gun. I dared anyone to talk to me again about my "behavior," I knew it all by heart.

I holed up at home to kill myself joint by joint. Until my tongue was worn down from gluing cigarette papers together, until my fingers crumbled from rolling them, until my smoke-filled lungs gave out. The outside terrified me. I had no place there and I felt too fragile. I felt under attack from everything.

I ruminated endlessly about my failed life and couldn't make any sense of it. I went back over all those years, turning them over one by one, and nothing made sense. Everything had gotten mixed up in my head and I was seriously close to madness, near total confusion. All I saw was my powerlessness and the extreme cruelty of people and life.

My mother, full of good intentions, drove me crazy with her administrative paper mill and her desire to see me move on. She didn't realize I was at the end of my rope. She didn't understand why I couldn't forget and why I always repeated the same things. She still couldn't admit what I had gone through, although that was all I asked: a recognition, an acknowledgement. She continued to act as if nothing had happened and it made me livid. She got the full blast of my anger, insults, and tears. I needed her but I hated her for not understanding me and I fled from her love.

Only one person listened to me and saw my suffering without flinching: Lyes's sister Insaf. Since the night I'd told her my life story, moved by her trust in me, she had become my most precious moral support. I noticed her sadness and felt her compassion immediately. "Shit, here I am living my quiet little life with my books and everything, and meanwhile there are girls like you living in hell! You know, Sam, I never saw that side of the projects. I'm realizing that, with my brothers, I'm really protected. I'm very lucky. I'm so sad for everything you had to go through! It breaks my heart!"

It was true that although we were the same age and shared the same ethnic background, our paths were completely different. Insaf learned about life from books, I learned on the street. Insaf was my friend, my calm harbor, my confidante, my support. She was the one who gave me the strength to live, the one for whom I wanted to bring my head out of water, the one through whom I became a better person.

After the terrible disappointment in Cyprus, she was at my side every night after her classes at the university. She was a witness to my slow destruction, but not one day did she stop believing in me. Each day, I offered her a cup of coffee and my tears. How I would have loved to offer her a smile! But I was incapable at the moment; I couldn't figure out how to get over this last slap in the face. I hated life and God for being so cruel. I blamed them for not listening to my prayers and not rewarding my efforts to get out of trouble. Was I going to keep paying all my life for having stepped out that night, lit up with pride over my shiny new Westons?

I'd been paying full price for nine years now. Nine years of trying to reconstruct the life, the being, that was destroyed. Nine years I'd been dying of pain. It'd been nine long years and it was like yesterday: still just as vivid inside me.

K. had stopped paying. He'd been free the last three years already. He'd "paid his debt" to society. I was still paying though. That was the kind of justice I endured. I'd been robbed of everything: my carefree youth, my love of life, my humanity. All that remained were tears and morbid thoughts to accompany each instant of my life.

Since my return I hadn't heard from Lyes. The last time I'd seen him was when I came to Paris to buy some pot. He was searching like a madman for a way to make some dough. He vaguely mentioned going to Morocco for someone, a plan that would earn him a little bundle. Yeah, right! I knew in a sec what he had was a rendezvous with ole Mary Jane—or dope to put it bluntly!

I hadn't heard any news because he'd been picked up and sent to prison in Spain. Insaf was the one who told me. It was a shock for me despite the distance that had come between us. Insaf joined me in tears now. I sent one, then two letters to Lyes. No response. One day I joyfully opened his first letter. Lyes announced to me that we were finished, that he'd had another girlfriend for the last six months, and that he didn't want me to write to him anymore. The other girl had slowly brought him back to life and would now take care of him. He loved her. I freaked out. Everything shattered around me. I couldn't believe I still loved him so much. It hurt, my whole body ached. My head buzzed with questions day and night.

I took advantage of this opportunity to destroy myself a bit more. I spent days lost in smoke and tears. I really believed we were meant for each other, even if we fought, even if we separated, even if, even if . . . We were meant for each other! Insaf took care of everything. She studied at the university, undertook administrative tasks for her brother, consoled her family, and always found time to be with me. Insaf was an angel. When she visited, we'd sit in my living room and listen to Mary J. Blige's *My Life* and cry, joined in pain. She cried for her brother and I cried over my life.

Winter passed. With the return of the sun and warmth, I recovered a bit of energy. My mother, who continued to bug me to get moving, succeeded. I landed a job as a lunch monitor in a school cafeteria between noon and one thirty. It was all I could handle. I liked being with kids, but I had to find the strength to put my mask on and it was hard. You can't fool kids. I tried to pay off my debt with my low wage. I hadn't paid rent in six months. I had to leave the place before the amount got bigger. My only choice was to return home to my parents.

The atmosphere there was very different. My mother had turned a new leaf. After forty years of a shitty life, tired of suffering and personal frustrations, exhausted by the tyranny of my father and boring jobs, she had finally woken up. She was fed up with constantly caring for others, sprinting between jobs and classes, with kids to drop off at daycare or school, and Sam in constant trouble—in short, with dealing with everything on her own. Sick to death of watching her life go by without any personal gain, she made a U-turn and walked out on it all. Except for my father, who was not about to let go of the goose that laid golden eggs! She wanted a life that matched her aspirations and her real self. After splurging on a trip to Greece, she fell in love with the country and decided to go work there. In order to settle there she took English and Italian courses, Greek being too difficult to master. It was a real challenge for a woman who had been forced to forgo school and be a homemaker. She spent summers as a seasonal worker in Greece in the tourist trade. She left for six months a year. Winters she spent in Paris. My father had been on unemployment for almost ten years. He had no more ambition or plans, no desire to do anything. He took care of my little sister when my mother was gone. He made her meals, waited to pick her up after school with a little chocolate croissant, helped her do her homework, and played cards with her. Life had sure changed! My other sister had gone away for health reasons for several years and only returned for summer vacations. I landed with all my baggage in the middle of their quiet little Eden. I was nervous as hell to be back, but I didn't have a choice.

Ever since Greece my mother had been harassing me constantly, she wouldn't give up! So I looked, and I found. A job as a counselor in a rec center for the month of August. During my first week my arm started to swell. I didn't worry too much about it at first; I chalked it up to roughhousing with the kids. A week later I couldn't move it at all. I went to the emergency room and the doctor's diagnosis was not encouraging: phlebitis in the left arm, and a near miss with a pulmonary embolism. I had to be hospitalized and there was no one to take me. My father and my sisters had left to join my mother in Greece. My case surprised the doctors because phlebitis usually occurs in the elderly. I understood that I was paying the price of a wasted life. Abuse of marijuana and alcohol, epileptic seizures, violence and suffering, disappointments and stress. I felt like my body had rotted inside.

I was very bitter. Each time I tried to get my footing, fate dealt me a slap in the face. I was tired of this dog's life, this constant exhausting struggle that always ended in failure. When I left the hospital, the doctors prescribed medication and advised me to stop smoking. They also suggested an arterial operation to prevent the risk of further phlebitis. I intended to take my medication, but stop smoking? Never! I didn't have the willpower. Dope alone let me put on my mask every day. If I had stopped, I would have burst like a grenade and littered the world with hatred. If I had stopped smoking, I'd have become dangerous and uncontrollable, I knew it. Even in the hospital, with an IV in my arm, I had snuck down to smoke a joint. . . .

Leaving the hospital, I felt like a bumper car at an amusement park, out of control and slamming into everything in my path. I couldn't control anything anymore, neither my nerves nor my addiction. All I could feel was my fury. I felt it blocking my throat and my stomach. It was my despair and my rage at not being understood that remained lodged in my body. They told me to move on, to forget what had happened, but damn! My life was a wreck! I was dead inside, how could I just ignore it?

My parents' unyielding silence left me in total disarray. How could they deny reality to such a degree? Why couldn't we ever talk about what had happened to me? They behaved like it was my fault. I was not guilty, though, I was the victim. Their lack of understanding made me degrade myself further. Told to move on, I moved on . . . toward my destruction, day by day, month by month, year by year . . .

I made a final stab at job training. I applied for a hip-hop jazz workshop with an American choreographer. For the audition, we had to improvise a dance. He walked among us making his choice. I felt frozen, incapable of showing him what I had. He thanked me politely. I refused to accept I'd failed and went back for afternoon auditions. I did not want to miss the chance to do what I love: to dance. When I was dancing, I forgot everything, and boy, that was what I needed. This time around, I did Liza Minnelli in *New York, New York*, the number I'd done at the club in Cyprus. He dug it immediately.

The workshop took place at a youth club in Saint-Denis. Mornings, we warmed up, stretching out. Afternoons, we rehearsed the choreographies we'd perform in six months in a hall in Vincennes. Once again I was hooked, but it was difficult. Facing myself in that wall-to-wall mirror was like being attacked. I couldn't bear to watch my body move and express itself. I felt naked. The gaze of others, and even their touch, terrified me. I was always feeling judged and attacked. I was not well, but I put everything into it. I had to do this show. I could then imagine getting a diploma in dance instruction. I started making plans, playing make-believe.

From the beginning of the workshop, I had three epileptic fits a day. The state of my body was beyond words with all the attacks I'd been subjecting it to for so long. Nevertheless, the sweat that poured out of me during rehearsal made me feel lighter. Evenings when I lay down to sleep, I felt a kind of serenity inside me. Truth was I was too wasted in every way to continue. Barry, the choreographer, realized this before me. "It's a crime to leave you like this and not say anything. You have to get help, Sam! You have to see someone about your epileptic seizures. You have a lot of talent, but you have to deal with your problems. You know what I mean? It'll take the time it takes, but it has to be done. OK?" He was right. I had to stop, it had to stop.

I'd been howling in my own way for years that I needed help. I'd been down and out for eons because no one had understood my plea. Barry was the first person to hear it and feel the distress hidden behind my facade. He saw the Sam who suffered, not just the street gangster or the artist or the thug I pretended to be. I dug Barry right off. I liked his enthusiasm, his contagious good humor, his direct, human touch. With him, I made unforgettable discoveries, African dance for example. We had the luck to work with Guem, a great percussionist. Both of us had extraordinary experiences, listening and feeling the music from within.

Unfortunately, the story ended there. All this richness was stolen from me once again. I felt a great disappointment missing this opportunity. I was ashamed to not be like the others and I especially felt rage for being penalized for something that was done to me. I was fed up with enduring, suffering, crying. I was fed up with being an open wound. Barry was right, no one could help me as much as I needed. I had to look for a professional: a doctor or a psychologist. If I didn't get help, I'd die of insanity and pain. I didn't give myself more than ten years to live in the state I was in. Alright, Barry! I'm taking hold of my suffering! I'm going to confront it—and bash its filthy face in!

21. Therapy

I'd reached the end of a long tunnel. I was twenty-four. Damn, it had flown by. For the first time I made a tally. Ten years had passed since that terrible night. I'd banked ten years of trouble, of loneliness, of slaps in the face. Reflecting on this, a deep feeling of powerlessness and injustice grabbed me by the throat. What a waste! Could I still do something with my life after such a massacre? Was there still a place for me in this damn world?

In the course of this self-examination, everything became clear, like the moon, long hidden behind clouds, reappearing suddenly and lighting up the whole night. My life, my anxieties appeared bearable now. I had a goal. I wanted to understand my life and cope intelligently. I'd look for and find someone skilled to help me. I refused to keep filling up this bag of woes that weighed heavier and heavier. I couldn't drag it around anymore. Thank you, Barry, for opening my eyes.

I turned to my general practitioner who had treated me for years. She had sent me several times to see shrinks. I had never followed up, too disappointed by their manner, their style, and their remarks. Very patiently, my doctor encouraged me to remain hopeful. "Don't worry, Sam, we'll find the right person." One day she received word a special service had been set up in a hospital for people who had been subjected to serious traumas. The consulting office was in Aulnay-sous-Bois, run by a psychologist. Without hesitating I called up and made an appointment.

The Aulnay Hospital was gloomy and at the reception desk I was sent to the psychiatric ward. Not a good beginning. It wasn't like I was crazy! Patients wandered like zombies in endless, gloomy corridors. I was scared of meeting a psychiatrist sicker than I was, like the kind who had sent me running in the past: messy hair, narrow glasses, haggard look, and nervous ticks. I had a moment of panic, but I decided to go through with it. I was right to do so. The shrink was young and pretty. She gave me a kind welcome and with a soft voice invited me into her office, as light-filled inside as the outside was gloomy. It was simply laid out without any fanfare, with a tennis poster on the wall and wall-to-wall carpeting.

I sat in the seat she offered and answered her questions one by one, a smile glued to my face to hide my inner chaos. Then the crucial moment came when she asked me why I'd come. I didn't know where to start. It was so complicated and confused in my little brain! I started to talk, and then it just spurted out. My whole life story came up in uncontrolled torrents, like I was vomiting a flood. I emptied my enormous reservoir of suffering and unexpressed words. I thought I had already cried all my tears but a flood streamed from my eyes while I spoke. I cried and I talked without an end in sight.

I sensed this shrink had a real ability to listen, and in her big green eyes I read a neutrality that encouraged me to let go. Then she made me face one of the white walls of the room. This wall, she said, represented the life I needed to face. "What the hell is this nonsense?" I thought. "The wall, life, what life? What is she doing there? She's playing with my head! What a mean trick! Whatever, look, don't make a scene. Do what she tells you, see where it leads!" I stood straight, facing the wall. She stood behind me touching my forehead with her cool hands and gradually tried to push me backward. My eyes were closed and I saw my life. I saw a film go by at full speed, a series of superimposed flashes. The faces of K., Jaïd, Lyes, my parents, images of Algeria, the trial I missed, etc. The images flashed by so fast I couldn't focus on any of them. All of a sudden I felt the need to run, head down, into the wall of my life. Like a bull, I tried to charge the barrier she had formed by placing her hands across my forehead.

After about ten minutes she asked me what I had felt and noticed about my body during her manipulations. I had felt an intense heat, like I was boiling inside. I sweated profusely, my T-shirt was drenched by the efforts I had made to break through the wall, my hands were hot and sweaty. I was amazed by all the feelings she made me discover in my body. I felt alive. Then she made me do a few breathing exercises. My chest was so tight that the breath passing through made it throb with pain. I kept trying nonetheless because I believed the air was killing the vermin in me.

There, the session was over, time to make an appointment for next week. "What should I do? Make another appointment? Go on! Give yourself another month, see what it brings!" I thought over what had happened as I left. In truth I had really enjoyed it. For ages, I'd been dreaming of someone capable of healing my mind and my body at the same time. I was so aware that the two were intertwined! I didn't know it was called body psychotherapy, but my whole being was craving it. Good, we'd see in a month!

After a month, I asked to come twice a week, so intense was the need I felt. It was only after several months that I got a picture of the huge damage that had been inflicted on me. I was in a terrible state. My body was stiffer than a rock and my head was pure fog. Having lost what was human in me, the being I brought to the sessions was a desperate, wild animal. But a stubbornly motivated animal! Questions flooded my mind after each session. I wanted to understand my childhood, my story, everything that had shaped my life before that dreadful night. Why had I preferred the street to home so early on? What had I been fleeing from at home? Why did I have two families, one in France, the other in Belgium? I wanted to understand why I was separated from my parents. Why had my father gone to prison? I wanted to understand the blurry images, the unexplained flashes, the whole unspoken past. To uncover it all, I wanted to harness my energy for a full-length psychotherapy. I felt a pressing need.

My decision upset my mother. She thought I was just stirring things up with all my questions about the past. I didn't hold it against her, I knew she'd had to bring me up on her own much of the time and she'd done what she could. She didn't realize her silence about my childhood prevented me from growing up. Nothing was worse than not knowing. By learning more about the early part of my life, I could better understand the rest. Her reaction didn't make sense. Now that I was trying to cope in an intelligent way, she didn't help me anymore than when I was banging against the walls. It was like she refused me everything: the right to suffer, the right to know, the right to make it out of that hell. As for my father, he couldn't have cared less. For him, I was just a wiseass, psychology was not exactly up his alley!

For more than two years I carried on a stubborn struggle to uncover the well-hidden past. I fished everywhere for information my mother refused to divulge. I understood that remembering those hellish years made her suffer, but I needed to understand, analyze, and accept them in order to build my life. I preferred this hard-luck story than nothing at all.

Three or four months after starting therapy, I had another streak of bad luck. I underwent left and right arterial bypass operations to prevent repetitive phlebitis. I suffered like hell from the two operations, screaming with pain night and day. Morphine, sleeping tablets, even joints didn't help. And I wailed with rage at being stuck in a hospital bed. How I would have loved to be living like others my age. It was like I was always paying twice for things I was the victim of, paying with the last inch of my own flesh. It was grossly unfair! I don't know where I found the strength to continue my analysis on that frigging hospital bed, but my brain kept chugging. I didn't let it slip. I wanted to make it out at any cost.

After two serious operations, I was given six months bed rest. I decided to make contact with my foster family in Belgium. I hadn't seen them since the rapes, which made it more than ten years. Now I wanted more than anything else to spend my convalescence there. When I arrived, I was happy to find that I still had a place at their table and in their hearts. Papa Jean and Maman Josette, after returning me to my parents, had adopted three children from India. First Toon, a handsome, brilliant boy, and then two adorable twin girls. It moved me deeply to see I was still their big sister.

Despite the tenderness I was shown, I still didn't feel at ease. Their perfect little existence, all rosy and full of affection, contrasted too sharply with mine. Watching them, I realized once again how gutted my life was. I dreamt of the little girl I would have become if I had stayed with them. What an awful waste! What sabotage! How unbearable to have these thoughts! It was like a punch in the stomach that took my breath away. But for six months the affection I received helped get me back on my feet and gave me the strength I needed to continue my analysis. I wanted to build my own garden of happiness.

It was there in Belgium that I got the idea to write a book. I wanted to leave a trace of my hard-to-believe story to help other girls. I had a great need to warn the little ones growing up in our projects. I wanted to make a book so that all I'd been through wouldn't have been for nothing. I wanted to tell others who suffered the same ordeal that there was always hope. I wanted to make it out of this hell and I would! I was certain of it now. During my stay in Belgium I tried to keep motivated, continuing my analysis on my own through writing. I didn't want to waste time. I had already lost ten years. I tried to make sense of my early childhood. The emotions were so painful, my thoughts got completely confused, but it didn't matter, the important thing was to write and empty my bag.

Since meeting Fanny, my shrink, my one goal was to pull through. My motivation surprised her a lot because it was not a common attitude among her patients. I wanted to scrub, clean, clear out everything inside me. I felt I'd chosen the right path and definitely the right person. I admired Fanny's skill. I could imagine how hard she had worked to reach such a high level of listening and responding. She was an intelligent and patient guide, and her interventions had a magic touch on me. Because, let's face it, I wasn't an easy patient. I arrived at her door in a deplorable state and every day I saw the distance I'd come. True, I participated and put everything I had into it, and my trust and motivation at difficult moments must have helped her.

Fanny immediately understood that my body had to speak

first. She understood that I would find no relief if we began with speech, which might have even made me more bitter. She chose to work with this body weighted down with layers of suffering over many years. A shattered, dislocated body in desperate need of relief. I could no longer stand straight, the weight of life on my back had become unbearable. It was like a shell of burning metal that made each step heavier. And then there was that ball of boiling magma bubbling in my gut. It kept me from sleeping, laughing, living. I felt it rise into my throat, strangling the cries before they could get out.

From the very first sessions, my body responded. First, by thoroughly emptying itself through vomiting and intense bowel movements. This lasted more than a month and would then manifest itself again during particularly difficult stages in my evolution. Then, my lower back began to reawaken through tugging sensations starting along the spinal column. Fanny explained that each part of my back represented a part of my life: the lower back was childhood, the middle was adolescence, and the upper was my current daily life. As I reflected on each part of my life, I felt my back loosen and relax through small, sometimes painful, spasms. I fully accepted these pains because I knew they meant freedom. Fanny helped me untangle my entire ball of grief and I could feel myself lose, little by little, the paralysis I was stuck in.

In the beginning the benefits of these exercises would last only an hour or so, then they persisted for two days. Now, they could last a week or longer. Through Fanny I learned to relax my mind, to really think, for my brain was a volcano in a constant state of eruption. Through Fanny I learned to analyze my stress and pain level. I also liked the way she talked and explained life to me. I could let my tears flow with her, and these tears made me more human each day. I charged like a bull toward understanding, my constant preoccupation.

This painful introspection was new. Everything that emerged amazed me. I went back through time. I dug in my memory for images and sensations of my early childhood, registered and then repressed in the back corners of my consciousness. I learned that each lived experience leaves an indelible trace in our bodily memory and in our life. I let all these emotions surge through my head and my body, then shook them until they first became understanding, then fully liberated words, thrown into the air.

I slowly realized that I was not responsible for the dreadful atmosphere in which I had grown up. I had believed for a long time that my misbehavior, my aggressiveness, and my ordeal were mainly to blame. I realized now they were reactions to the violence that had already been inflicted on me. I remembered the beatings, the gobs of spit, the insults, and the contempt that were my father's sole modes of relating to me. I had a truckload of horrendous memories of him. I could see him drunk, for example, running after me with a butcher knife. You don't forget that.

I also learned to accept that my mother was an unconscious victim. She was totally incapable of saying "stop" to my father's excesses. She could only submit to him or run away. She had been trained in submission since early childhood. Running away was an answer she chose when she went to Greece. I could see that not only was my violence not the cause of the atmosphere at home but also that it made perfect sense. I was right to fight back, I was right to resist their "education," their mentality, their way of life. Why should I have accepted the consequences of their mistakes arising from their own immaturity, my father's prison time, my stay in Belgium? Why should I have resigned myself to my father's beatings and the excessive demands of my mother concerning the housework and babysitting chores? Not only did I carry my burden, but they also forced me to carry theirs.

Because their suffering was too heavy, they denied it, and to do that, they had to deny me too. I was especially sensitive, and I felt their unacknowledged pain in place of them. They never understood this and spent their time trying to silence me. By the same token, they also silenced everything alive and healthy in me, my kindness, my spontaneity, my joie de vivre. Now I could see all the violence and denial I had been through coming to the surface. When I came home after each therapy session, with my consciousness awakened, everyday interaction with my parents was difficult.

22. Let's . . . Drop It

As usual my mother kept nagging me to find a job. She didn't understand the interest and importance of my work with Fanny, or the state of exhaustion in which this work put my body and my mind. I still didn't feel ready to tackle a normal life in society. I knew myself, I knew to what point my behavior could put me at fault. I was already suffering from trying to build a life without reference points, support, or the chance to talk over my efforts. It took me ages to understand that I wouldn't get any help from my parents and my morale was sunk in a feeling of deep loneliness.

To make my mother happy, I found a job as a counselor in a rec center in La Plaine-Saint-Denis, a rough neighborhood where the standard of living was very poor. Despite the poverty, there was a lot of solidarity in this neighborhood. The kids I worked with were all still small and adorable, but already little devils. I liked the girls and loved my work, but I encountered big problems with the educational staff. The volcano in me was still active and I exploded at the drop of a pin. I was always feeling snubbed. I still thought every person I met was a potential enemy, someone capable of doing me harm. To disguise my fear, I used my big mouth and it was not always appreciated by the other counselors, or by the supervisor, who was always on my case.

I didn't talk like a counselor, I didn't structure my activities well, but I worked hard. Still, my supervisor nitpicked over every little professional failing for months on end. She drove me crazy till I quit, disgusted. Another disappointment for me. I started to ask myself if I belonged in this profession or in society in general. It presented an opportunity to tell my mother that I wouldn't look for work as long as I was not psychologically stable. I learned to say no to her. I wanted to continue my work with Fanny at my own rhythm. I couldn't fight on several fronts at once. Nor did I want to fail again.

A few months after my operations my mother decided to sue for financial damages. Since I couldn't go to the trial, she thought a settlement would help me rebuild my life. To do this, she contacted the agency for assistance to victims in Pontoise, where the trial had taken place. No doubt it was her way to make amends for what she hadn't done ten years earlier. Still, I appreciated her gesture toward me, something my father never tried in his life.

There wasn't much hope of winning because the case had long been closed. Normally, one has two months after a verdict to undertake such an action. But nothing stopped my mother. Sure, she was loaded with ambiguity, but she wouldn't quit. Me, I was annoyed to have to make contact with another lawyer, to build up yet another case, this time with all the prescriptions and medical reports: EKGS, scans for the epileptic seizures, psychiatric hospitalization, years spent homeless and adrift. By necessity, my mother dragged me into this process, but I drew the line when it came to going to Pontoise. That place held too many bad memories for me. I wouldn't go until the day of the hearing, it was the most I could stomach. Since I didn't have the means to pay a lawyer, I requested a court-appointed attorney. I was given one in Pontoise. It was my mother who made the trip to talk with her. I wrote her a letter to express my sincere desire to be present at the hearing, giving her all my reasons. I added that it was now the one place left where I could tell my ordeal before a court of law.

After months of waiting I learned that my suit had been dismissed: it had been filed too late. I had expected this, so I wasn't surprised. My mother was absent when I got the news, gone to her summer job in Greece. So I went to the lawyer to pick up the papers in my file. She told me "of course, as she expected," our request had been denied. I understood in a flash that she was biased and never put any effort into the case. Her attitude made me tense up. Without much conviction, she suggested I make a last attempt at the court of appeals in Versailles.

"Yeah, well, guess that's what I'll do, take my last chance!" Her distain for me spooked me so much I had to respond.

"Aren't you brazen!" she said. "It's government money you're wasting!"

"Oh really? You're the one wasting government money doing shit! I'm through with the good manners, give me my file back, I'm outta here!"

When I get personal, it's 'cause I'm pissed. That's the signal to take off before I lose it completely. She watched me leave like I was some kind of alien. But who was the real alien there, huh? For an extraterrestrial, that meuf rocked! Truth is I was jinxed when it came to lawyers. She was the second one to take me for a ride. From her comments, I understood she hadn't made a decent presentation of my case. For her I wasn't worth it. She must have gotten next to nothing to plead my case since I was getting court assistance. But was that a reason to treat me like shit?

For me it was truly a double standard. I was penalized because I didn't have money. Useless to talk about my disappointment and the rage festering in my heart. I hadn't been very motivated about this trial at first; now nothing would stop me. The way that lawyer behaved, the way she talked, the way she held herself and looked at me had frankly lit a fire under my butt. She thought she could pull a fast one on me! To think that she hadn't even lifted a finger to get to know me or understand my story, and that she had taken no account of my request to be present: see you at the hearing!

It was summer. I'd spent the month of July working in a rec center and now vacation was approaching. It'd been ten years since I had a vacation. My mother invited me to join her in Greece, in Mykonos, with my little sister. I didn't even remember what a vacation was anymore and I couldn't get over the beauty of the island. And Mykonos is a gorgeous island. Sunsets there take your breath away, the narrow streets and white cottages reminded me of the Kasbah in Algiers, back in its heyday. However, seeing people all happy made me feel rotten, like there was a gap between me and everything else. I couldn't laugh and act carefree when I was feeling black inside, when I was still trapped in a bubble of suffering. I couldn't take advantage of what presented itself. So I lost myself in books. *The Alchemist* by Paulo Coelho was a revelation to me. I learned I had to make my own heroic legend. I was like the shepherd who, to reach his treasure, undergoes all sorts of ordeals. I too had trekked over treacherous paths and crossed deep oceans where I almost drowned. The treasure I wanted to reach was life. Real life. That was my path, my destiny, my personal legend. Thank you, Paulo!

Among her clients, my mother had a Parisian lawyer who spent his vacation every year in Mykonos with his family. He was a corporate lawyer and didn't deal in criminal law. Back in Paris she contacted him and explained my case. Very kindly, he agreed to take a look at the file but didn't promise anything. His approach was touching: he wanted to meet and talk with me. During the interview he explained that my case was not easy because of the statute of limitations, but that he'd do some research. "Listen, we have a million in one chance, but a chance nonetheless, and I'm willing to try it. We're going all the way, agreed? If it doesn't work, we'll go to the European Court of Human Rights!"

Finally! Someone who took my story seriously! His optimism and his support helped me believe in the trial. During the interview I observed him a lot. I could trust this guy. He was an honest type, listening to everything I said, calm and energetic. He was a class act. "But to do this we have to build a rock solid case and have an expert demonstrate why you didn't take action before. We're going to try to explain that you were in no state to act and that you did not know there was assistance for victims, OK? You're going to meet a very good friend of mine, a very well-known psychotherapist, who knows how to build a case because she's got lots of experience working in court."

This lawyer grasped my situation perfectly. He understood my distress and how I'd lost faith in the justice system. He invited me to come see him often. He wanted to get to know me better in order to defend me. He called and sent me letters to explain each step he took. He didn't want to let me down and I was very touched by the cautious, constant regard he had for me. Moneywise, he told me we'd see about that later, after I had won the case.

I kept going to Fanny. It'd been three years we'd been working together. My recovery was slow and painful. But I felt changes happening in me. I'd take fifteen steps back, then twenty forward. But in the end I moved ahead. Fanny was a huge support. I learned to channel anger, to resolve conflicts, to take time to reflect instead of reacting with my gut or my heart. I learned to become a real human being in my professional and family relations. I felt stronger, wiser. It was the person inside me I was building step by step. I wanted to go as far as I could in understanding my story and give birth, finally, to the person hidden within me for so many years.

Fanny only treated me with her touch and with her words, never with medication. Since starting the work with her, my epileptic fits had ceased. I didn't need them anymore, my pain had finally been heard. I still hadn't quit pot, but I was considering it. It was part of my plan. Fanny supported the lawsuit but put me on guard. She didn't believe in recovery through money. I didn't understand her point of view right away and this first disagreement troubled me. Nevertheless, she continued to offer her shoulder, even in this effort.

The psychotherapist the lawyer sent me to, his friend, happened to be the shrink I had gone to see with my mother. The one who had cost too much. It seemed no coincidence! I finally got the feeling that luck was on my side. During the first meeting she remembered me perfectly, my bruised eyes, my story too. She wanted to see me several times to better understand my story and be able to describe my reactions to the series of assaults I had undergone. A report was needed explaining why I hadn't taken action at the time of the events.

Doing all this made my head spin. . . . Giving account after account, explaining why, where. . . . I felt like I had to justify myself for something done to me. Like I was a charity case. My mother believed the money would help me get back on my feet again. I wanted to believe her, but I couldn't forget Fanny's warning. I tried to understand what she meant by it. But my need for recognition and my thirst for justice were so fierce that, despite her reservations, I charged ahead.

I was twenty-five. Another year bagging a ton of emotions. I couldn't count the times I had wanted to end it all, to throw up my hands and run, to quit trying to understand everything or improve my situation. How many times I'd rather have checked out for good than break my head on all this crap. I had to fight on every front: assume responsibility for my life, my story, rebuild myself, try to make it professionally, give testimony for the court report. . . . There had to be some smidgen of happiness out there after all that!

I had gone to Fanny to free myself from my past, most of all from the rapes and their aftermath. It was weird but I couldn't get myself to speak about it. A million times I told myself as I got there, "OK, today you talk about the rapes!" But she still only knew the broad picture. Once I was with her, there was always something else that came out of my mouth. We'd built a strong connection, but I still felt too ashamed to talk about it. I was scared of what look she'd give me, and of disappointing her with my mess ups in the past. I also sensed that talking wouldn't suffice to empty my baggage and extinguish the volcano that had been burning inside me for so many years. I didn't want everything to be laid out, cleaned up, understood, and dissolved in Fanny's office. I wanted to leave a permanent trace.

At night, in bed, the idea of writing a book quietly took root. A book where I could retrace my steps, explain to everyone close to me what I had gone through, and tell all those who never believed in me to shut their traps. It was too much, I couldn't stay silent. It would have been too easy. Back then I was so eaten up by my thirst for justice and recognition that I wanted the entire world to know what I'd been through. And no one in the media had yet spoken about tournantes. The shrink who had written the report on me understood this yearning. She suggested I appear on a national talk show on the theme "Is there life after rape?" I was contacted by a journalist prepping the show for the host-producer. She invited me to talk about my ordeal. I agreed to meet her but I reserved the right to decline. First I wanted to talk it over with Fanny. I'd watched the show a bunch of times. It was interesting, but it raised questions. What kind of image would people get of me? Would I be able to deal with the looks people might give me in the hood after they had seen it? What would I gain from this show? Would I feel better after I'd blown up on TV? I was as packed as ever inside, crammed full, I might blow up more than talk, which would totally exasperate the TV host.

The journalist invited me to the studios to work on my reservations face to face. She was young, perhaps younger than me, the typical Parisian "trend" girl, as one says. The expression makes me puke. Despite our being the same age, we lived in two worlds diametrically opposed. I introduced her to mine. She chimed in with "What did you feel at that moment? How did you react? Why this, why that. . . ." I felt more and more queasy and started to have all kinds of suspicions: I didn't like her, she didn't respect me, she was hassling me. . . . During the interview she "suggested" I not mention anything about girls getting dragged into tournantes, about the reality of life in the projects, the missed trial, or the association to help children that helps no one, because it might shock the viewers. Nor did she want me to mention the crap with the lawyer. I started to ask myself why I was there. Sure, I wanted my testimony broadcast across France, but not at any price and not with this journalist. I didn't trust her. I had only been contacted because another young woman had declined at the last moment. They were trying to replace one pawn with another on their crappy chessboard! I also wondered what state I'd be in after this testimony. It was a question that didn't concern the journalist.

Inside, I didn't feel strong enough or rehabilitated enough to face a situation like this. I didn't feel like showing myself all teary eyed, pathetic, and pitiful. I wanted to protect myself. It was the first time I felt this way, and it marked a big step toward self-respect. But there was another thing. It was a show for a national audience, presented by a well-known TV host who earned top dollar from his shows. In other words he made money off other people's problems. What a racket! My viewpoint may have been shocking, but if anyone was going to make dough off my story, it was me. Certainly not that host, who couldn't have cared less about my life. Only thing he was concerned about was his audience rating.

The journalist took the cake when she asked me if she could come film my family, my theater classes, and my sessions with Fanny. The brat was totally getting on my nerves now. I kept quiet, I didn't want to look like a wild beast. She didn't get the picture, in any case, she was too lost in la-la land. Frankly, I didn't see myself with a camera aimed at my ass, trying to explain the sad life of a ghetto chick. And there she was telling me that they were going to give me a makeover, a hairdo, that I was going to be super pretty! She actually thought she could turn me on with her "mouthwatering enticements." What was I, a moron?

Leaving the studio, I had the rotten impression I'd been taken for a circus animal. I hurried to see Fanny and gave her the low-down. She flipped. She was not happy her colleague hadn't called her before proposing this crap to me. Besides, she didn't need this kind of publicity to make her office run. Bottom line, there was no question of that psychologist and the media being allowed to cash in and sabotage the psychological gains we'd made over the past three years. She thought an experience like that could scuttle the still-fragile foundation we'd laid. It could do a lot more harm than good. Plus, she had no desire to scrape me up off the floor in pieces. "If you have such a strong desire to tell your story, write your book!" she urged me.

Fanny's anger and arguments were a huge wake-up call. I landed back in my boots with a thud. What a relief! My doubts and suspicions were right on and Fanny came to my rescue again with sound advice. So I called up the journalist to decline her invitation and explain my reasoning. She was not happy.

"Oooh! Now, that's not very nice! You're the second one to decline at the last minute! I don't have anyone lined up now."

"Uh, yeah."

A big, empty "yeah." I didn't see what else she expected me to say.

"Can't you make an effort? Trust me, everything will go fine. A taxi will come pick you up, there'll be a big buffet here with Danish and drinks, then we make you up, style your hair, you'll love it. And Jean-Luc is super nice! After the show you'll be chauffeured home. . . . See, you're wrecking it for everyone. . . ."

Whoaa! What frigging good did it do me that Jean-Luc was super nice? She had heard nada, she had understood nada about my reasons. All she wanted was to wrap up her show, find enough interviewees to make the housewives weep. "Listen up! I never promised you a thing!" I answered her. "I told you I'd talk with my psychologist first before making any decision. I don't feel ready to face all this. And anyway, the day after the shoot, I have to attend a hearing at the court of appeals in Versailles and it's too much for me. Have you even considered the state I'll be in after your show? Who's going to pick me up and put me back together again? Won't be you!"

I wanted to testify in a carefully thought-out manner. No way was I putting myself at risk. TV is just a circus, anyway. Did I want to be fed to the voyeurism of the media lions? The journalist wanted to hypnotize me with her sequins and spotlights. She thought I was gaga about going on TV. She really took me for a moron. I was not after pity. I wanted people to wake up and understand things they'd previously been unaware of. They could make the show without me.

This experience strengthened my desire to write a book. Each word would be chosen, mulled over, allowed to ripen. The book would hold the weight of what I had lived through, the value of my reflections, and my drive to make it out. It would leave an indelible trace of my experiences, and I'd finally be able to file my past away on a library shelf.

23. "First, I Want to Thank the Honorable Judge . . ."

—

Today was a big day for me. I was awaited at the court of appeals of Versailles. With me were my mother and my littlest sister, who was skipping school today to give me moral support. Lots had changed at home. My parents were divorced. My mother had finally managed to get the divorce she'd been clamoring for forever and the mood at home was way different. The heavy, suffocating atmosphere had given way to the sunshine hidden in my mother's heart.

My problem had become something shared with the whole family and we spoke about it openly. My little sisters tried to understand and give me support. They'd gotten good grades at school in spite of all the family troubles. These years had been hard on them too. I had woken up in a calm mood and tried not to put my head in a vice with a million questions. I just kept repeating a little speech in my head in case the judge asked if I had anything to say. The lawyer had said, "It probably won't happen, but. . . ." This "but" told me anything was possible.

My name was written on the courtroom door. "We made it, Sam, we made it! How long have you been living in hell? How many years have you been waiting for this?" A big, fat thirteen. Today, you could turn the page on those thirteen years. Be courageous, stay calm, say what you have to say, if you can, and please don't cry! These were the thoughts going around my head at this moment, which I'd waited so long for. Fanny was there too. She didn't approve of my mother's initiative and all that went with it, but she wanted to come to support me anyway.

I tried to stay calm and wait my turn. I hadn't smoked a joint that morning, I wanted to keep my head clear. Only the attorney and I were allowed to enter the courtroom. Waiting for our turn, I watched the jury, which was made up of only women. Would that play in my favor? Who knew. I hadn't had luck with the two women who had represented me so far. I heard my name called, it was our turn. The attorney looked at me and smiled to show me he was on my side. We both stepped forward. Usually, when a case is presented in the court of appeals, only the judge, the assessors, and the attorney have the right to speak.

Before the attorney's opening statement, against all expectation, the judge asked me if I wanted to say something. I answered that I would prefer to speak afterward. During the presentation, I listened closely to what was said. I couldn't help but cry when I heard the account of my life. The attorney, with simple words, knew how to describe the long tunnel I had gone through. With accuracy and precision, he described each stage of my life. He, at least, didn't try to pull one over on me. Then it was my turn to make a closing statement. I thanked the judge for authorizing me to speak. Then I took the leap.

"First, I want to thank the honorable judge for letting me speak. I am very aware today that there is no question of retrying a closed case. I was fourteen at the time of the events, I'm twenty-seven today. These thirteen years have been long and painful ones. I began psychotherapy three years ago to try to free myself from my past and find some happiness. I think I'm on the right path. I want to move on and start a new life. I ask you to excuse me for crying, but I am overwhelmed to be here. Today, I've got lots of plans including, especially, working toward a diploma in youth education. I'd like to lead art classes. There are lots of other projects I hope to carry through with. I hope for your understanding and support. Once again, thank you very much for letting me speak."

Enough! Tears were streaming down my face and I was too overwhelmed to continue. I thought I was done anyway. I'd said everything. Not in the right order, but that didn't matter. I thought the big ball of misery that festered in my gut was going to pop out finally. I thought it might explode, jump out of my mouth, like I'd been dreaming of forever. But no, nothing of that sort happened. In any case I was proud of myself for having overcome my fear and controlled my emotions. It wasn't easy to speak in front of those people and summarize years of hell in five minutes. I was happy to have not cried about my fate and for emphasizing the positive aspects of my rehabilitation. Now I had to wait for the result of the deliberations that would come in several months. I had already waited ten years, it was only a few months more. What a torture, this Justice thing!

After quitting my job, chilling and smoking joints, and taking a vacation in Mykonos, I signed up for a training program in Montreuil for a diploma in youth education. A while back I had mentioned this plan to my supervisor at the rec center in La Plaine, who had laughed in my face. Well, just you wait, sweetie! Last year I had had my nose in the trial, but this year I'd show what I was made of and I'd earn that diploma, which would be the first of many goals. Thanks for laughing in my face. Got me moving! And then, one fine morning, the telephone rang. It was my lawyer.

"I'm happy to announce some good news, Sam, you won your case, and the aid for victims fund has awarded you damages of one hundred thousand francs."

"For real, I won? They believed me?"

"You know, the day of the trial, I felt the judge had a real sensitivity for your story, but I didn't want to give you any false hope. You were very good that day. What you said was really great, I mean it. Well, I'll do what's necessary so you can have the check as soon as possible. Go treat yourself to that dream vacation you've always talked about!"

"You bet! That's exactly what I'm going to do. But, wait. What about your fees? Shall I make an appointment to come in and discuss it?"

"I was glad to meet you and to be involved in this case, but I prefer you keep the money and invest it in all the things you couldn't do when you were young, like you told me about. What you went through was horrendous and excruciating and you were particularly courageous. Today, you deserve some peace."

I had no inkling he would make such a generous gesture. For a moment I was speechless, and it was with a voice overcome with emotion that I answered, "I thank you from the bottom of my heart."

"Gook luck, Sam!"

"Thank you, thank you so much! You didn't have to, yet you spent so much of your time. How can I thank you enough!"

"Well, we'll see each other in Mykonos next summer, right?" he said as if we were old buddies.

195

"Right, in Mykonos, and thank you."

Happy Birthday, Sam! I turned twenty-seven that day, what a birthday present! I had won my case! Good, now for the diploma! Messing up at La Paine-Saint-Denis had really trashed my self-esteem and I was having a hard time getting back on my feet. It was tough. Staying seated, writing, listening—it all felt light years from me. My application was accepted, though, and I started the training course in Montreuil. The year promised to be good. I had made the cut, I had won my case, and I was planning to spend New Year's 2000 in New York City. Whoopee!

One evening after class, returning home on the RER, I had the misfortune of wanting to rush like all the office workers in a hurry to get home. Running to get on a train before the doors closed, I lost my balance, twisted my ankle, and fell flat on my face in front of a cop in uniform. I was so embarrassed about falling that I went to sit in a corner to assess the damages. My ankle was all swollen and started to hurt like hell. What a jerk! I hobbled home on one leg, quite an athletic feat. Once home I took off my sneaker and saw with horror that my ankle was a bruised mass of flesh. I tried to assure myself that it wasn't too bad and called a friend to take me to the hospital. Diagnosis: plaster cast and three months sick leave.

NO! How could anyone have such rotten luck! What was happening? All the gods on earth were against me! I wanted to blow my top, but at whom? At the god of the RER, the god of the rushing crowd, or at the god of some crazy comedy show? Goodbye America, goodbye New York! Goodbye dream vacation!

I tried to negotiate for something other than a cast. I explained to the doctor that I'd just begun a training program, that I couldn't go on sick leave. I explained that it was an ambition I wanted to fulfill at all cost. It was something I just had to do. It was an intensive training program lasting six months. There were still three months left for me to cram and give my best. It was a gamble I intended to win. Friends in the program were understanding, they took turns bringing me the work so I could study at home.

At the end of my convalescence, I rolled through class like a billiard ball on a pool table. I was pumped to the max to make up for lost time. I had several exams to pass. First, I had to be evaluated on my artistic aptitude, then on my pedagogical skills with children in rec centers. I still had to get certified in CPR, then pass the final exam, which included a written term paper. I was worried sick about the first exam, because I lacked any education in painting, either practical or theoretical. Unlike most of my colleagues, I hadn't visited museums, and I knew nothing about art history. On the other hand, I painted by instinct. I fiddled around, but with my whole heart. My high school diploma in decorative arts counted for zero compared to what the others knew. To my huge amazement I passed the first exam, which meant my artistic aptitude was recognized. Encouraged, I promised myself that I'd fill in my cultural gaps later.

For the second exam, I had to show my skills with a group of children. The center where I was interning had been preparing a theater piece since the beginning of the year on the theme of "musical forms of the century" with dance and drama. Each age group participated on this project and the show was to be presented to their parents at the end of the year. I took on several jobs. I led a workshop on theater games to help the kids feel comfortable on stage. I made costumes, directed, and together with another colleague, worked out the final choreography. The supervisors appreciated my work and my ideas. I felt recognized and fired up with energy. It was a real pleasure to create and guide. I realized through this that I could concentrate, show competence, and follow things through. Finally, for the evaluation on activity management, I organized a competition for the show poster. The winner's poster would be used to publicize the show. The examiners came to evaluate me during this activity. I was judged on how I ran a workshop, on motivating and managing a group of children. My stomach was in my throat, I was so nervous.

I passed the test. It was almost too much! I attained the CPR certificate with no trouble, only the final exam remained. I had to write a term paper. It wouldn't be a piece of cake; I had never written anything in my life. I had to come up with fifty pages explaining why I had chosen this career. I toiled day and night to get it done in time, with the help of Insaf. I was so busy I didn't notice the time go by and when the test results came in I was surprised.

"On your mother's life!" The words shot out of my mouth before I could hold them back. The instructor had just announced that I'd made it. I couldn't believe it, I was crazy happy. I had won my gamble, I had gone all the way, in spite of my handicap at the beginning! It was no Ivy League diploma, but it was totally wild for a little street punk like me who never listened in class. Self-satisfaction is a delicious feeling! I laughed so hard it nearly cracked my face. The days following this news, I swam in a kind of euphoric joy. I had never known such a high. Case won. Diploma awarded. What could keep me greeting life with a smile?

Against all expectation, these successes—the case, the diploma, and the zeros that garnished my bank account—didn't make me happy. I came to the painful conclusion that the trial had not given me my dignity back. My malaise was still present. My ball of misery too. It had shrunk, definitely, but it was still there, festering in my stomach. It still stirred in the midst of my happiness. It bled into everything, annoying and blocking me from moving on. Did that mean Fanny was right? She had let me search. She had let me try things out. I had tried many escape doors. They hadn't been the right ones, or at least, they alone weren't enough. I knew what door could really deliver me now. My deliverance would be this book.

Epilogue

MY BOOK

It's four in the morning, and I've just written the last word of my manuscript. I can barely believe it. I've actually gone the whole way with this dream, I've written my book. I thought books had to be written by really cultivated people, and I, the little hoodlum, have done it. I'm so worked up I feel like going down into the street and running around waking up the whole hood, ringing at doors and intercoms and climbing up to the windows and banging on the glass to tell all the sleepers: "Hey! Know what? I just finished MY BOOK!"

I want to assemble a huge Parisian crowd and scream out my crazy huge joy. I want to share this deliverance with someone. I open the window. The night is deep. Silence reigns. Not a cat around. What a bummer! Seated in my chair, enveloped in silence, I let myself sink back. A rush of emotions floods over me. Everything swirls. Tears stream down my face and I don't try to wipe them off my cheeks, I let them be. They are tears of relief, tears of deliverance. They feel right. For a second I fall into a void. A deliciously comfortable void, an absolute serenity. Unforgettable feeling.

I look at the thick ream of paper on my desk and find it hard to grasp that I've done such an enormous piece of writing and thinking. I've succeeded in bringing this adventure to completion, extracting from my memory and my guts the heavy story held back so long in pain. I needed all those years of rehabilitation in order to be able to recount my life story without destroying myself in the process. It was when I told Fanny I had finished my book that I realized what that meant. As usual, my body spoke. I felt a big bubble of air rise from my stomach and pass out of my mouth. My voice was hoarse and my jaw ached. Then tears popped out. A feeling of relief washed over me. So there, that was it, it was all over, it had all been said, it had all been put behind me, right?

My bag of woes doesn't weigh me down anymore, now it weighs two hundred pages on the table next to me. I can feel I'll need time to live with this new reality. That frigging bag made me suffer like hell, and I'd gotten used to it. It was like a second skin protecting me, a thick shell. It was part of me. Without it, I feel weak, all new. I can no longer claim to lack self-awareness. I know what I'm doing and because of that I can see the life ahead of me. I'm still a little lame duck, though, landing on a new planet called "Real Life," who has yet to learn to trust her destiny.

I didn't want my story to stay secret, in Fanny's office. To overcome my woes I went through years of effort and lots of suffering. Would it be fair to let the ones responsible for this waste sleep tight? Should K. and his guys, the lawyer, the association and the social services, and my parents be allowed to sleep tight? It'd be too easy for everyone if I stayed quiet, if I found a way to smile and have kids and not say a word again! No, I was splitting the bill. No reason for me to pay the whole check. Since no one ever wanted to hear me, they'd read me instead! I wanted to hit everyone between the eyes with what I'd suffered through all those leaden days. I wanted each of my emotions to slice right through them, like I was sliced through with their stupid mistakes.

I didn't want vengeance. Such a desire had left me long ago. What I wanted was for each person to realize the part he or she had played in my nightmare. I was sincere, I was lucid, as much as I could be. I wanted to show how the negligence of my family, my close ones, the lawyer, and social services, all had beaten me down, on top of the trauma of the rapes. This book was about my truth. And if I didn't express the truth as others saw it, it was quite simply because that wasn't my goal. I hid nothing, especially in relation to my parents, and I knew there would be a price to pay. Maybe they'd forever turn their backs on me. I was ready to take that risk.

During my therapy I found myself in front of a door. It was the door that opened to an understanding of my parents' attitude. I opened that door and took a step. I discovered their suffering. It was so huge they couldn't even face it. Then I wanted to try to go one more step toward them. That was when I found out that the effort should not come from me alone, that I'd gone my part of the way. I had to make the decision to close that door again and save my own skin. It was a horrible decision to make, because I had to mourn a dream, the one of feeling close to my family.

The trial hadn't freed me. I was heard, I was definitely recognized. They even gave me a hundred grand. The story could have ended there. I could have been pleased with my diploma and the dough and started a new life. But I understood that I couldn't get there until I had emptied my bag for good. Only at that price could I recover my dignity. My path, my personal story, was my book. Once, during a session, Fanny felt that it was the right moment to introduce Josée. She'd already talked to me about her when I had expressed my desire to write a book. I needed someone solid and able to be in sync with the work with Fanny. That was what I found. I showed her the pages I'd jotted down in Belgium. She decided that I should write it myself and that she'd take on the task of restructuring and reshaping it. She assured me she'd support me throughout the writing process, through her questions, sometimes hard, and her encouragement.

I trusted Josée right off, and without hesitation, I dove into my abyss of troubled waters. I spent whole days scribbling away in an attempt to understand my nightmare and its consequences. As I wrote, the painful memories rose to the surface. The reflections they trailed made my body react, like in therapy with Fanny. Each week, when I wrote, my body made itself heard. I felt a very strong sensation of pressure in my throat and jaw. Like invisible hands trying to strangle me. It was the words and emotions locked in my throat that needed to be set free. My stomach prompted me, my spine and my ball of anxiety too. When I took the pen up, each time this parade of pains accompanied me and wouldn't let go until the end of the now familiar process. When everything had been spat out and written down, clarified under Josée's eye, reflected on anew, it was finally digested and integrated. Then it all started again, fed by new elements. It took time for things to ripen in me and for the meaning of every step to become clear.

Gradually, everything was released and put back in place like the pieces of a puzzle. I recovered my memory and I was able to situate passages in time that had previously lost their order. I unearthed horrible memories I had repressed, and they took on new meaning in light of the way I was currently heading. I devoted an entire year to the book and it would have been impossible to work simultaneously on anything else, in a job, for instance. So as not to get completely lost in the writing and the reflection, I had to learn to manage my thoughts, to clear my mind, to relax. Cooking and reading saved me from becoming overobsessive.

Each week, presenting my work to Josée was a big deal. I dreaded it. I had to get over the shame of showing myself naked, as I really was. Her way of listening, her questions, and her reactions gradually changed my self-image, corroded over the years by the people around me. An image that stirred up guilt and shame, suffering and hate, and that unbelievable feeling that I deserved what I had gotten. Getting back what I had written in typewritten form, clarified and restructured, helped to strengthen my awakening consciousness. I existed as did my woes. Josée gave me a new way of looking at myself, a true way that I instinctively came to trust. She saw me for what I am and gave me the esteem I couldn't manage to give myself. At no time did she allow me to debase myself. The interest and esteem she held for me often blew me away and made me cry. Soft tears, a balm for my shattered heart. Tears of healing, a precious gift for the abandoned child I had been. Tears that made me feel a burgeoning love for myself, a shy compassion for the heroine of this insane tale. The connection between us was intense. I got constant support, far beyond the work on the book. Right up to the end she was there, right up to the end she kept her faith in me. *Merci.*

With this book, I could feel I recovered a form of dignity. Until now, not a day went by that I hadn't thought about being humiliated. I had lost it royally each time someone talked about rape in front of me. Today, even if I hear the worst crap about this subject, I keep my calm. I let people spout their junk. I don't consider myself "Sam the street scum" anymore or "Sam the rape victim," and I don't present myself as such, after years of it seemingly being stamped on my forehead. For years, I seemed to define myself in terms of the terrible things that had happened to me. I don't need my victim ID anymore, now I exist in other terms. I am Samira, I am twenty-nine. I believe in life and I want to be happy. I have done what I needed to have a chance of succeeding.

POSTFACE TO THE FIRST EDITION

I wish to state that everything I have written in this book is scrupulously accurate. I have exaggerated nothing. Neither have I allowed my judgment to be clouded by any bitterness resulting from the suffering I have undergone. I know the banlieue. I have lived and hung out there for more than fifteen years. I know what I'm talking about.

I'm tired of hearing people say that the problem of gang rapes in the projects has been exaggerated and that tournantes are sex games in which girls participate by consent. No, the savagery I have described is a reality that has claimed many victims, of which I am one. Nevertheless, I don't reject the world in which I've lived and in which I became battle hardened. I still live there and work with kids there. I feel attached to the projects, their working class warmth and richly diverse cultures. There are plenty of terrific people in the projects trying courageously to succeed, for all the guys there aren't rapists, far from it! The banlieue can be like a big family, with its constraints, its gossip, its special codes of honor and forms of solidarity to match every challenge.

"If you're short of something, socks or whatever, no problem—things are always falling off the back of trucks!" "If someone tries to pull a fast one on you or your sister or your cousin, no problem—someone else will also get into a scrap on your behalf." "If you're feeling down, no problem—there's always someone around to crack jokes, have a smoke with, and laugh till you split your sides." That's all part of the banlieue. It's a world of all or nothing, the best and the worst. What I've recounted here is the worst—so bad that it turned my youth into a living nightmare.

POSTFACE TO THE SECOND EDITION

When my book came out, I had no pretension about stopping gang rapes. As if writing a book could put an end to violence of this nature! I just wanted to break the law of silence and elicit an awakening of conscience in our moms and our dads, our brothers and sisters, our neighbors and our cousins, male and female, in Paris and across the rest of France. In fact I wanted to reach society as a whole, to break this law of silence that causes us so much suffering and with which we've lived for too long.

The day after my first appearance on a TV show, I was scheduled to work with my kids at Franc-Moisins. All night I psyched myself up to face their collective judgment; in other words to confront eyes that would now be transformed for the occasion into laser beams, ready to slice through me with dazzling destruction.

Armed with mere sunglasses, I prepared to throw myself into a new battle. To my utter surprise, the anonymous hands stretched toward me simply wanted to give me a big hug. The looks I was thrown were capped by respectful smiles. I heard a lot more "bravos!" than I expected. At one point during the day, I encountered a young guy: hooded sweatshirt–gym shoes–backward cap, the kind the media typically call "the new gangbangers of the banlieue." Wouldn't you know, he gave me a shove in the tramcar! I told myself all those open arms and smiles for me were too cool! I got into attack mode to destroy him with my "fire-lancer," (i.e., my big mouth). But all timid and small voiced, he looked right at me and said, "Hey! The way you talked yesterday was killer!" I frankly admit that for a nanosecond I felt like a bitch. And by the time I realized it, unfortunately, the tram doors had slid shut. I barely had time to give him a smile of thanks. Coming from one of those kids often labeled too fast, his words had really touched me. A remark like that gave me a boost of hope.

And after that, each time, every spontaneous gesture of sympathy I received threw me for a loop. Same as the piles of letters sent to my editor blew me away. After being on the invisible side for so long, finally this sunlight of full support made me feel good.

Then, one day, during an interview a journalist told me about the Fédération Nationale des Maisons des Potes, a federation of associations working for better conditions in the banlieues, and about its president, Fadela Amara. My first response was, "Me, I'm not your association type, and if it's about learning to bake cakes or square dance, doesn't interest me." But for once in my life, chance was on my side. A little while later, in my weekly pile of mail, I got a brochure about the federation, explaining all the work the girls associated with it had accomplished in three years. Pushed by curiosity, I read the whole thing. And I suddenly saw that I wasn't alone or, rather, was no longer alone. Our conclusions about the situation of young women were identical: the improvement of their situation and their role in society has yet to be undertaken. And don't even talk about the situation of young men. . . .

So, one night we got together for couscous at Fadela's. Chatting about this and that, she told me about the Women's March against Ghettos and for Equality and how the preparations were coming together, and she asked me to be what they called its godmother. I agreed with great pleasure but also with pride. The march, which attracted huge media attention, lasted over a month and stopped in twenty-three locations in France. I took part in several stages of the march, which helped me realize how many women and men are interested in our work and its significance. It was also beautiful to hear how tongues were freed up along our route, even if what they revealed to us was permeated with all kinds of suffering.

The demonstration ended on March 8, 2003, International Women's Day. That day I finished what represents a first step for what lies ahead at the Place de la République—dig the symbolism—surrounded by all my girlfriends from our association against violence toward women, "Ni putes, ni soumises" [Neither Sluts nor Slaves]. Fadela held my hand tight because she knew how a big crowd like that intimidates me; there were upward of thirty thousand people!

All of us were ready and determined to lift up our heads and to never again accept living under a dark sun. All were ready and determined to stop this gangrene of suffering that has been eating away at our neighborhoods and imprisoning us in a mental ghetto.